YOU'RE ALWAYS BEING INTERVIEWED

How to be Intentionally Extraordinary

RON BRUMBARGER

abbott press

Abbott Press books may be ordered through booksellers or by contacting:

Abbott Press
1663 Liberty Drive
Bloomington, IN 47403
www.abbottpress.com
Phone: 1 (866) 697-5310

ISBN: 978-1-4582-2057-8 (sc)
ISBN: 978-1-4582-2056-1 (e)

Library of Congress Control Number: 2016917751

Print information available on the last page.

Abbott Press rev. date: 10/27/2016

CONTENTS

For my extraordinary wife Cindy

And for my two boys, Hudson and Tanner -

May the nurturing and godly wisdom we've
sought to impart to you encourage
You to always be intentionally extraordinary in all you do.

ACKNOWLEDGEMENTS

Much of this book is centered around the ideas of values and morals. In this book, I explore the importance of respect, of authenticity, of grit and giving it your all. You will read plenty of stories about people who possess a strong moral compass who are intentionally extraordinary. I want to thank my parents, Jack and Deana Brumbarger, for the ability to understand, demonstrate and teach intentionally extraordinary behavior and character. I do not believe I could have written this book, with so much of it dependent upon an understanding of character, without the upbringing my parents gave me.

Many thanks to my loving wife, Cindy, who tolerated my thousands of interruptions this summer for feedback on a paragraph or a sentence. Thank you, Cindy, for being so encouraging and supportive of me while writing… even during our month-long, 6,800-mile RV trip to the West Coast. Most importantly, thank you for being such a great, godly, role model of character and authenticity to our boys and me. I love our sharpening of one another and hope you'll see our countless hours of conversations about raising men of character well represented in this book.

May my boys be as fortunate as me to have such thoughtful and nurturing in-laws as Jim and Dottie Meyer. The faith, values and character demonstrated by them and instilled in Cindy have served as a compass and roadmap to me for many years. Their influence runs deep throughout this book.

With so much of this book centered around deep values, I was confident I had the right assistant in Isabella Penola. The rich values, ethics, and rigor instilled in her by her parents, John and Lora, made teaming with Isabella an easy decision. I'm thankful to them for their dedication to raising their children in such a way. Of course, I'm thankful for my assistant Isabella too! Without her, within these musings, you would frequently experience first-hand my easily distracted mind. I fully intend to be Isabella's campaign chair someday when she runs for President.

Nowhere is attention to detail more pronounced and imperative than in writing a book. My close friend and world-class attorney Robert often says to me, "Look, I need you to focus!" I'm the benefactor of many years of wise counsel from this man. Admittedly, focus and details are not my gifting. As such, it is crucial to surround yourself with exceptional talent. Two bright young ladies, Grace Murrell and Faith Murrell, were instrumental in the intricacies of editing this book. My dear friend Jennie Thomas graciously edited and shared her grounded insightfulness and wisdom to ensure the stories herein hit the mark. Katelyn Harbeck's twenty-something perspective gave us a fresh and invaluable lens through which to look at these stories. The well-trained eyes of Angie Murrell helped put the polish on the final edits. They, along with Isabella, ensured a clean manuscript.

Throughout this book, you will enjoy the fun sketches by Grace and Faith, intended to help you remember and visualize some of the more remarkable stories.

The *You're Always Being Interviewed* website[1] and photography associated with this book are the work of a bright student enrolled in Apprentice University, Justin Dickey. I hope you enjoy his remarkable creativity and talent as much as our editing team did. Nice work JD.

Some of my close friends graciously permitted me to interview them to gather wisdom and help embellish a point made in the book. Their

---

[1] www.yourealwaysbeinginterviewed.com

expertise is second to none on the specific subjects I asked them to consider. If you know them, you know what a blessing it is to have them as friends. I'm very confident you'll enjoy the ideas and insights shared by my friends Wil Davis, Nikki Lewallen, Dennis Dunn, Mike Alley, Kim Stoneking, and Erin Albert.

The positive stories bolstering the lessons in this book wouldn't be complete without my friends permitting me to reference them. Their stories of being intentionally extraordinary demonstrate a job well done and one we should all seek to mimic. They include, Angie, Bjorn, Brock, Cindy, Emily, Emily, Hannah, Hudson, Isabella, Josh, Keith and Darla, Lora, Paige, Rebecca, Sutherlin, and Tanner.

Finally, thank you to the countless mentors and Talent Spotters who have actively and intentionally instructed me over the years. There are far too many to name. Their examples of strong moral character helped spur the writing of this book.

FOREWORD

Some tasks in this life are worth considering and other tasks determine your worth because you were considered for them. It is a great joy and honor to have been considered worthy of writing the foreword for such a unique and much-needed work as this. In *You're Always Being Interviewed*, Ron Brumbarger brings to the surface cutting-edge solutions that are warranted in the gap between theory and practice. It is no secret that academics, many with little or no hiring experience, have filled individuals with philosophy and impracticality on so many levels that the practical requirements on day one in seeking and finding a job are almost nonexistent. To this problem comes the solution of a placeholder or finishing school.

Looking at my own journey as a first generation immigrant who landed on the shores of American opportunity, I wish this primer had been available for someone like me. To learn about the importance of consistency and to hide my desire to offer qualifications that were not required would have been invaluable. As I read the chapters, I was more convinced than ever that if we offer these principles to everyone who is looking for an edge, the book would have done its job and the author would have found his audience. However, I would like to go a step further and hope that this book is given to everyone in the finishing stages of their formal education as a guide that can help them leapfrog the competition and gain a visible advantage in the race of life.

To you, the reader, I would like to encourage you to have a note-taking device in hand and use it to personalize and internalize each principle and process as it is offered. This collective dissertation on your own part will become a road map where the suggestions and solutions will give you a clear and decisive picture that will prepare you for every encounter. In addition, I think that every time one receives practical advice, it would behoove them to immediately find an avenue to teach it. This forces consistency on your part and keeps you grounded in being a constant student. I am sure that *You're Always Being Interviewed* will get you where you need to be. Good luck and God bless you as you unpack the knowledge and translate it into wisdom so you can arrive into the tomorrow of your own life with the worth that you created for yourself.

Krish Dhanam
Managing Partner Skylife Success
Corporate Evangelist and Business Philosopher

INTRODUCTION

First off: contrary to what the title might lead you to believe, this book is *not* about interviewing. It's about how to be interviewed without actually being interviewed.

That is probably (scratch that, definitely) confusing, so let me clear it up. I subscribe to the motto, "When you least expect it, expect it." Your actions and attitudes when you're not "on" for a potential employer indicate who you really are. Employers and mentors – whom I like to call "Talent Spotters" – know this. Talent Spotters know the best indicator as to who you really are and how you will actually perform under their employment isn't always evident during an official interview. The 'you' presented in casual conversation, in your character when interacting with others, in your general manner of conduct is – when you least expect it.

Talent Spotters know the best indicator as to who you really are and how you will actually perform under their employment isn't always evident during an official interview.

In my many years of experience as a Talent Spotter, I have come to learn the incredible importance of a first impression. Sometimes, you only get one shot to show another person who you really are, and it's vital that the 'you' they see is marked by strong character.

In this book, you will find a plethora of stories from my own experience of working with and meeting individuals – for whom I have used their real first name - who positively exemplified what it means to be intentionally extraordinary. Conversely, I will tell you some stories about people who, well, just missed the boat. As you encounter these somewhat confounding stories, I encourage you to place yourself alongside me and experience these scenarios first-hand. I will try to bring some levity and memorability to these stories. These examples – for whom I have used fictional names – I affectionately refer to as my Cast of "Knuckleheads." These stories, while amusing (and sometimes baffling), are also somewhat disconcerting, as it's troubling to think that people really act in such a way. And in case you're wondering, yes – *all these stories are true!*

I surely can't be alone with my Knucklehead stories. If you're a Talent Spotter, I'd love to hear those stories about the interesting people you've encountered. You know, those stories that make you just shake your head. You can submit your stories on the *You're Always Being Interviewed* website.

When you demonstrate to someone your strong character, trustworthiness or overall competence, you are making deposits into your relational capital account with that person. If your account balance is high with another person, it enables you to have confidence when asking for favors, and the other person knows that yours is a relationship worthy of an investment.

The Knuckleheads do an excellent job of demonstrating what it means to destroy relational capital or blow an opportunity. Let me take a minute to explain this idea of "relational capital." Whenever you interact with others, especially in a business or networking setting, you build "relational capital accounts." When you demonstrate to someone your strong character, trustworthiness or overall competence, you are making deposits into your relational capital account with that person. If your account balance is high with another person, it enables you to have confidence when asking for favors, and the other person knows that yours is a relationship worthy of an investment. This is the entire premise for why you're always being interviewed. Your interactions with another person automatically increase your relational capital account with them, or reduce your previously-stored balance.

Your relational capital account not only matters to the person with whom you share the account, but it also matters to everyone within their circles. If I ask a previous employer of yours whom I know and trust – someone who has a high relational account balance with me – whether or not I should hire you, what will they say? The state of your relational capital account with them directly impacts the state of your relational capital account with me.

While all of this might sound pretty serious, writing this book has been exciting. I have enjoyed chronicling these stories for you. While writing, I had numerous opportunities to share my enthusiasm with friends. I quickly noticed a somewhat disturbing trend – fidgeting! My friends would fidget and primp while I described my book. Some even changed their eating habits knowing this book was in process for fear of being a story in this book! They were worried I was interviewing them. Okay, I admit, in some cases that was true, but most often not so much.

Earlier this summer I attended an outdoor graduation party with many of my friends. I had the opportunity to share my excitement about this book with a dear friend named Kate. Kate is a poised and well-spoken young lady and a very busy mom of three young girls. She was wearing flip flops. (I share this detail only because it becomes important, as you'll soon see.) As we sat talking about how much we appreciated the young graduate, Kate was pretty relaxed. There was a natural pause in the conversation, so I mentioned I was writing this book. Kate, in her naturally eloquent fashion, asked what the book was about, the title, etc. As I proceeded to describe this book, I noticed Kate rolling her toes under her flip flops and fidgeting a bit. Knowing Kate pretty well, I simply furrowed one brow and tilted my head while looking at her.

She promptly stated, "I didn't have time to paint my toes this morning before the party and I mistakenly wore flip flops…"

Sorry my book title made you uncomfortable, Kate. I do hope the nail polish gift basket I gave you helps minimize future fidgeting. Here's to many more graduation parties together without any pretense. Thanks for making for a great introductory story in my book.

In all seriousness, several friends have asked me if I was concerned about my friends "expecting it" when we meet. I sure hope not as that's not my goal for this book. So, when we as friends are hanging out for coffee or watching a football game, chill… please!

This book is *not* about being judgmental and critical of every action. I'm not always judging other people, especially my friends – I promise! After years of being a Talent Spotter, I simply have seen too many mistakes repeated too many times, and I feel a duty to share the basic things you can do to stand out from the pack.

In closing, this isn't about interviewing, nor is it about being judgmental or fidgety. It's a roadmap to being intentionally extraordinary, to behaving with poise, grace, and discipline in a way that positively and memorably conveys who you are to acquaintances, associates and potential employers. I hope you enjoy the book – and more importantly, I hope you learn something!

CHAPTER ONE

CHARACTER

CHARACTER

O n the wall of the conference room at our Bitwise Solutions offices hangs a framed list of the firm's core values: a collection of terms and definitions identifying qualities and character traits each individual employee, and the company as a whole, strive to embody.

Having a set of values clearly laid out helps our firm to maintain an identity grounded in strong character. Acting in accordance with those values not only helps our own consciences and eases our own operations by decreasing drama and stress, but it also helps us to represent ourselves well to clients and the community at large. We want our actions to be marked by integrity and our reputation to be linked with strong moral character.

That same principle of demonstrating rich character and developing a reputation marked by that character applies not only to a company, but also to an individual. When you're talking to a teacher, a college admissions officer, a potential employer, someone who might connect you to a future employer, a Talent Spotter – anyone – you are going to be judged right off the bat not by your abilities but by the kind of person they intuitively perceive you to be. As the saying goes, you have one chance at a first impression (more on that in a later chapter), and the best way to make a good first impression is not to act like a great person just in that moment of meeting, but to simply continue your normal, well-practiced behavior of being an individual marked by strong character.

In this chapter, I'm going to delve into some crucial character traits that I'm looking for whenever I meet a new person I'm thinking of hiring in the future. These traits are good to practice developing no matter what, but their presence or absence in a person is easily noticed and remembered by a potential employer.

A Good Listener

Poet Maya Angelou declared, "I've learned that people will forget what you said, people will forget what you did, but people will never forget how you made them feel." There's a good chance you know someone who, inexplicably, makes you feel comfortable. When you talk to them, you feel heard. When you share things with them, you feel like they genuinely care and are engaged, and because of this, you're more likely to seek them out, trust them, and remember them in the future. Good listeners make an indelible mark on one's memory – positively – because they make one *feel* appreciated. Good listeners are noticed and remembered.

> Good listeners make an indelible mark on one's memory – positively – because they make one feel appreciated. Good listeners are noticed and remembered.

In most cases, you can tell whether or not someone is a good listener pretty soon after meeting them. Last year, I gave a talk to a group of about a hundred students at Anderson University, in a bowl-shaped auditorium designed so that I felt incredibly close to, almost face to face with, the students. Yet, out of those dozens of faces, there was one girl who sat eye-level with me who was obviously focused throughout the entire talk. Her body language sent the message of, "I care, I'm engaged, and I'm processing everything you're saying." Her attention level was intentionally extraordinary. There was no fidgeting with her phone or chatting with her neighbor. At the conclusion of my talk, I told the students the thesis of this book – that you're always being interviewed – and that I had been "interviewing" them all throughout my lecture. Based on her poise, facial expressions, and attentiveness, I knew this young lady was fully engaged and that she would meet with me during the networking sessions afterwards. Good listeners are desired, they are obvious, and they are remembered.

Integrity

Wil Davis, a veritable fountain of wisdom, a man of strong character, and a dear friend, said to me, "There has to be congruence between your actions and your words, and if there's not, the words are worthless. In one word, that congruence is integrity."

A few years ago, I coached some students at a local university on a large project. While doing so, I overheard one of the students suggest to his peers that they ask his buddy from the previous year's class for a copy of his project, from which they could base their project. The student didn't know I was listening, and he acted in a way that demonstrated his lack of integrity. I'm quite confident his university would not condone such behavior.

Your integrity is judged, however, not only by your own actions, but also by the actions of the people around you. If people know that you associate (or connect your social media) with individuals of questionable ethical behavior or backgrounds, they will think of you in the same questionable light. Conversely, if you associate with people of good standards and morals, this will reflect well on you. You will be seen as principled, polite, and well-behaved if you associate with those who are principled, polite, and well-behaved.

While I'll go into more detail on this in a later chapter, I would be remiss if I did not mention social media here. A teenaged employee

3

for the high school student-led division of Bitwise Solutions was once fired for demonstrating a lack of integrity on social media by posting inappropriate pictures of himself engaging in illegal and immoral activity. Before you post anything, ask yourself: Would I want a future employer to see this? Is this positively reflecting my character and exhibiting strong integrity and character?

While writing this book, I had the opportunity to have breakfast with a long-time friend of mine, Mike Alley. Mike is currently the chairman of Patriot Investments here in Indianapolis, and in the past, he's served as the commissioner of the Indiana Department of Revenue and as the President and CEO of Fifth Third Bank of Central Indiana. Needless to say, he's experienced in recognizing the kind of people with whom he should and shouldn't engage in deals, and he places high value on a person's integrity when making such decisions.

Mike told me a story about someone who came to him seeking an investment in a new start-up. This person had previously been a customer of Mike's bank, and Mike remembered that he had not been regular about paying his bills and handling his affairs. Mike told me, "It was an interesting opportunity and my former customer was going to be an investor. Another guy, a friend of mine, was actually going to be running the business. I really liked him and had a lot of confidence in him. Ultimately, I did not invest in the business, not because it was a bad idea or because of the management team, but because I knew the track record of one of their investors – my former customer. There were just too many red flags. And now they are embroiled in various lawsuits between the shareholders."

As Mike said, "It really is true that whatever you're doing now is going to make an impression that some future interaction may bring about." Your integrity and honesty are always being judged. If your first impression – whether it involves actions done in person, via social media, or by the company with which you associate – is tied up in things that lack integrity, your character will immediately be judged in a negative light.

So, simply put: Be good, and choose to be around those who are also good!

Trustworthy

If we think of "integrity" as meaning that someone is of a strong moral fiber, trustworthiness can be thought of as telling someone that you need something done by Friday and knowing that, when Friday comes rolling around, the task will be complete. There isn't any extra stress in worrying or wasted time in reminding. I don't have to micromanage and check back in to see if it's going well.

There is nothing like a trustworthy team - one that you don't need to double-check. There is an incredible peace of mind that can be found in knowing that your staff is made up of individuals you can count on, and so when I'm looking for a potential employee, I'm invested in seeing that they exhibit signs of trustworthiness. A simple indicator of this is that the person has proven to me that they'll follow through without my needing to check in – that they reply to emails in a timely fashion and follow-up with introductions and scheduling of meetings without prodding.

That may seem like a small way of seeing whether or not someone is trustworthy, but that is how you build trust: slowly and gradually. Sometimes, you really have to build that "trustworthy account" up by proving your trustworthiness in small tasks over a long period of time. There's an excellent example of this in the Book of Matthew in the Bible. Jesus tells a parable of a man who entrusted differing amounts of money to three of his servants and instructed them to manage it as they saw fit. Two of the servants traded wisely, invested their money, and doubled their amounts, but the third only dug a hole and hid his money in the ground. When the man came back to collect his money from the servants, he praised the first two for being prudent and trustworthy, while scolding the third for not acting as a good steward.

As the man said to the first two servants, "Well done, good and faithful servant! You have been faithful with a few things; I will put you in charge of any things." (Matthew 25:23). Trust is built just like that. The more you prove yourself as trustworthy with smaller things, the more you'll be trusted with in the future.

> *The more you prove yourself as trustworthy with smaller things, the more you'll be trusted with in the future.*

Kim is a great example of someone who built trust over time. I met Kim at a school event some time ago. My first impression of her was that she was pleasant and trustworthy. The next day, I received an email from her – also gracious and polite – expressing her pleasure at meeting me and inquiring about a comment I had made about needing a little help around the office. Soon, Kim was managing small tasks as my assistant, and as time went on, I began to trust her with more and more. Fast forward eight years, and Kim is my go-to person who, in a lot of ways, runs the day-to-day operations of the office. I know I can trust her to manage entire tasks, relieving me of a lot of stress and worry because I have confidence knowing that if Kim's on it, it's in good hands. Neither of us expected that the rich role of responsibilities she has today would begin with a simple encounter at a school function!

Complete trust means never having to look over your shoulder to ensure someone is doing what they are supposed to do. Such is the case with Lora. Lora was hired a few years ago to manage the finances of a non-profit for which I was the board treasurer. Month in and month out, Lora's diligence and hyper-attention to details gave me assurance and confidence in her work product, but more importantly, in her trustworthiness. She built a very large relational capital balance with me. Later, when I started Apprentice University and needed someone to manage our back office operations, my trustworthy "right

> *Repeated deposits of trust in relational capital accounts result in rock solid, steadfast relationships.*

arm" Lora was not just on the list of candidates, she *was* the list of candidates. Lora, whom I mention in the acknowledgments, epitomizes trustworthiness. Repeated deposits of trust in relational capital accounts result in rock solid, steadfast relationships.

Lack of Hubris

Every so often you encounter someone who, at first glance makes you think, "Hey, this guy knows what he's talking about…" That is, until you spend a little more time with him.

A few years ago, I served on a board of a rather large non-profit and I was asked to chair a very significant committee. My committee was responsible for managing the finances and investing the assets of the organization. After several very successful years of operations, we decided to add new members to our committee because the workload was increasing and we needed more perspectives on the tasks at hand. As our work was intricate, delicate, and highly confidential, we decided it would be best to interview a few candidates for our open seats.

Let me introduce you to Jared. Jared was a guy we were interviewing to join our team. Coincidentally, his background and resume suited one of the open positions at my firm quite well, and I was genuinely excited to get to know him. Jared seemed like a really nice guy. I was eager to add his contributions and talents to my committee. My committee's work was taxing and required close attention to detail. Generally speaking, the complexities of the work required new committee members to spend several months getting up to speed before they could add genuine value.

The unwritten and unspoken rule is rookies start making measurable contributions after about month three. At the 30-minute mark of Jared's *first* meeting, he showed his true colors. He halted the discussions and, while looking down his nose at us, proceeded to admonish us about how flawed our processes and policies were. Not that we weren't open to fresh ideas, but Jared's condescending attitude caught us all off-guard. Jared subsequently tamed his arrogance a bit, but the other committee members never trusted him again.

I could have done a better job vetting candidates and Jared was evidence of this. I sure learned my lesson! Unbeknownst to Jared, he was being interviewed, albeit passively, by me for one of our open positions at my firm. I had even shared his name and background with my team, excited to ask him to consider one of our open positions. Obviously, Jared was never invited to interview at my firm for a position he never knew was an option for him – opportunity lost.

Teachability

Jared's disposition, attitude, and hubris confirmed to me that he was completely unteachable – moreover, that he was disinterested in learning. In today's society, it is imperative to maintain a *learning disposition* at all times. I love the often-heard advice of "Learn something new every day and go to bed smarter." A learning disposition ensures one maintains a teachable attitude and seeks, processes, and evaluates new information constantly. We've all met the antithesis of a teachable person. I call them the Unteachables. Remember the "know-it-all" guy in school? He knew, and made sure everyone was aware, that he had the answer to every question before the teacher finished asking it. Not only was he difficult to work with on a project or class play, but he was simply difficult to be near! Don't be an Unteachable!

> *I love the often-heard advice of "Learn something new every day and go to bed smarter."*

Teachability starts with humility and is mastered through a learning disposition. A learning disposition is a mindset where one embraces a cycle of *study, try, fail, adapt, master... repeat.* In this mindset, we enter each situation knowing we are going to first *study* the case, apply our discernment (more on this later), then use our knowledge and experiences to take a first step and *try* what we believe is the obvious answer. Note, we started off with a studious attitude because of our learning disposition, not the *perfected* solution. Unteachables lead with their rendition of the perfected solution before studying the situation. Approaching each situation with the intent of studying first and preparing to fail ensures we maintain a teachable attitude.

Study → Try → Fail → Adapt → Master →

Let's dive into the components of the learning disposition cycle.

Studying starts with the ability to listen with an open mind. An open mind is one ready to receive new information and new ideas and to think divergently. An open mind is willing to challenge the status quo while respecting the lessons from history. Much more than just research and a few Google searches, studying means to be intentionally of a mindset to gather new knowledge. Thinking divergently while studying, especially new subjects, enables us to see things we might otherwise miss.

Trying our hypothesis and expertise as a solution to a given challenge is a quick way to test and evaluate what we know, or what we think we know. You may have heard the phrase "fail fast." Failing fast has two wonderful outcomes. First, it limits the cost of time, capital, and resources chasing down the wrong trail. Second, it gives us the opportunity to fall back, learn, analyze, and try again with a slightly different strategy. When it comes to trying, I like the analogy of riding a bike. When my boys were learning to ride a bike, they studied how others rode their bikes and, with a little coaxing from me, they gave it a try. Sure, they fell and skinned a knee or two, but the reward of sailing into the wind on their new bikes far outweighed the cost of failure. In fact, they fell over and over again.

Failure is a critical element of learning. In 2015, at Apprentice University, we started The Failure Institute with the tagline, "From oops to epic, there's value in failure." The Failure Institute's mission is to learn from mini case studies of other's failures. While there's value in learning from our own failures, harvesting knowledge from the failure of others is in our best interest. Through The Failure Institute's work, we glean, catalog, and analyze the key elements of these case studies in failure. The plethora of wisdom gained through these case studies is invaluable. Most importantly, understanding these failures ensures we do not repeat the same mistakes.

Adaptation ensures we are gathering input from our senses and surroundings, rapidly processing our understanding of that information and making course corrections accordingly. Driving a car is a fitting example of adaptation. The roads we drive on are seldom straight and, at least in Indiana where we enjoy the freeze-thaw cycles every winter, rarely without potholes and bumps. As you drive down the road, you are making mid-course corrections all the time. You adjust the wheel ever so slightly for undulations in the road, bumps, curves, and obstacles along the way. You cannot drive a car and keep the steering wheel in the exact same position the entire time. This simple yet commonplace scenario teaches us a lot.

First, when driving, our senses are on high alert (or they better be). We are watching our surroundings, listening for noises, and constantly measuring whether things are the way they ought to be as we drive down the road – our feedback loop. Second, because of this feedback loop, we are constantly making micro changes in our course direction. Finally, those pesky potholes represent the unexpected variables we are certain to encounter along the way. The little ones aren't such a threat and we can compensate for those, but hit a big one and it may be game over.

Mastery of a subject, task, or art implies we can execute the task with excellence routinely. The likelihood of failure is nil. In fact, once we have mastered a task, it simply becomes second nature. It's ingrained into us like muscle memory. Take, for example, mastering typing. It's likely that learning to type for the first time was maddening, right? You were forever hunting and pecking for the letter Y, confident it was on the bottom row. After a while, you trained your mind to know exactly where it is on the keyboard. The connection between the brain and the fine muscles in your fingers, after hours and hours of typing, slowly start to eliminate the need to hunt and peck.

Mastery follows rigor. Remember the first *Karate Kid* movie? That movie is chock-full of great elements for metaphors in teaching (and my students are sick of them, I'm certain). In this movie, Daniel is the new kid in school and is bullied by some thugs. He's a smaller kid and doesn't have any self-defense training. One night, Daniel encounters the thuggery crew who are preparing to beat the daylights out of him. Suddenly, they are interrupted by the appearance of this seemingly old man known as Mr. Miyagi. Mr. Miyagi puts a halt to the pending beating poor Daniel was about to endure.

Fast forward a few minutes to one of the most memorable movie lines ever created – "Wax on. Wax off. Wax on. Wax off." (Bet you made little circles with your palms facing outward!) Daniel is being trained, through repeatedly waxing Mr. Miyagi's car, in the value of rigor and patience. Rigor, patience, and practice are the key ingredients needed to master a given subject. The mental durability lesson taught to Daniel through days of waxing Mr. Miyagi's car over and over again ensured he would be emotionally and mentally prepared for the challenges he would subsequently encounter. Mastery ensures we can successfully complete the assignment before us with ease. Through all that work and practice, Daniel remained teachable.

Malleable

In our hyper-competitive, fast-paced, knowledge-based economy of today, we must be on guard to maintain a learning disposition, avoid becoming an Unteachable, and remain malleable. Unteachables frequently use words such as *always* and *never*. Unfortunately, the Unteachable's expertise on a given subject is quickly obsolete as things change so rapidly. What was locked away as truth, a constant, or a fact, may be unknowingly challenged, disrupted, and replaced in a nanosecond.

Unteachable's expertise on a given subject is quickly obsolete as things change so rapidly. What was locked away as truth, a constant, or a fact, may be unknowingly challenged, disrupted, and replaced in a nanosecond.

I have enjoyed the incredible honor of mentoring Josh for the past nine years. Josh is a very bright young man. I first met him when he was about 15 years old, and I've worked closely with him through thick *and* thin, good *and* bad. He understands teachability and the learning disposition cycle. I hired Josh numerous times over the years while he was in high school and between semesters in college. A few years ago, I asked him to take on a very audacious project. His summer job was to create a software product plan around a concept that was nebulous, esoteric, and vaguely defined. He was but nineteen years old at the time and the project seemed, on the surface, way out of his league – and it was.

Josh's teachable attitude and desire to learn ensured I had the right guy. There is no way an Unteachable could have ever handled this assignment.

They would have begun with, in their minds, a perfected product plan, omitting all market research, conceptualization, prototyping, and feedback. Josh, on the other hand, began his challenging summer job by asking questions. His questions would lead to more questions. He was in the study phase of the learning disposition cycle. About mid-summer he reached a point where he could *try* our concepts out on a few trusted friends. He failed miserably…down in flames. That failure was immensely valuable in helping us better understand the marketability for our fledgling product.

Fearing he had disappointed me, Josh humbly asked if he should abandon the project and look for another summer job, but I could tell he wanted to give it another try. Booyah! I couldn't have been happier. This young man was right where he needed to be – frustrated, persistent, eager to learn, and eager to please. My edict to Josh was: get back on your horse, learn from your failure, and try again. Little did he know, I was looking for his reaction to what I was pretty confident was going to be a failure, much more so than a successful product introduction. Later, I shared this with him. His raised eyebrows and body language told me that he didn't expect that!

Ultimately, our crazy software product idea didn't launch. It was way too far ahead of its time and the state of the art in technology, but I consider Josh's summer experience a major success. Teachability and a learning disposition often lead to conclusions we may not like nor want, but the journey of getting there is a cornucopia of learning opportunities. Missing those learning opportunities along the way would have resulted in a failed summer experience for Josh.

Josh has developed a great sensitivity for maintaining a teachable disposition. In his young career, he's had numerous opportunities to work with many from the Unteachable tribe and he knows how to effectively handle working with them. We recently had the opportunity to grab coffee, a treat of diminishing frequency with my young protégé. He shared how he seeks to preserve a teachable attitude and practice the learning disposition cycle. He's now mentoring some men younger than himself, discussing and demonstrating the tenets of a teachable attitude, while sizing them up for their summer jobs. I bet they didn't expect that.

Edifying

"Edify" comes from the Latin *aedifico,* meaning "to build; to create." And let me tell you, it's a lot more productive – and a lot more fun – when you're surrounded by edifying people who have a constant mindset centered on building and creating with enthusiasm. These are the people who always push a little farther, always expand the dialogue a little more.

> *It's a lot more productive – and a lot more fun – when you're surrounded by edifying people who have a constant mindset centered on building and creating with enthusiasm.*

How does this come out in a first conversation? A simple example is the "tough question" scenario – one that will inevitably arise in an interview at some time or another. There are two ways to answer a tough question. One is by simply answering yes or no. Another is to go beyond that and answer with "No; however, if I think about this a minute, maybe we could do this instead and that might be a better way to resolve this problem." If you merely answer yes or no, the conversation is over. As an interviewer, whenever I get a yes or no response, I feel like asking, "Okay, so… why?" Without elaborating or delving deeper, you're not building or edifying the dialogue. Instead, strive to help elevate the intellectual state of the conversation and make the conversation edifying to both parties involved by making an effort to build. Your effort does not go unnoticed.

Confidence

The character trait of confidence, when coupled with humility, a teachable spirit, and a desire to be edifying, results in a keen self-awareness of your abilities and knowledge. It's important to recognize that while you won't know everything and have the answers to everything, that does not mean that you should clam up and not participate (that isn't edifying!), nor should you demonstrate ignorance by trying to assert a fact that you don't understand (that shows arrogance!). Don't be too eager to share, but know that you should and are capable of speaking *with* confidence if you *have* confidence that you *are* confident in your understanding of the subject at hand.

Having confidence means that you accurately understand your level of experience, knowledge, and skill. You don't sell yourself short, but you also don't boastfully act as if you are the most equipped person in the room. Look around and smartly realize that there are individuals in the room who are probably more experienced in the subject, and see it as a great opportunity to learn from them – listen, ask questions, show that you are interested and desire to improve. Others will remember you for your well-placed awareness of your abilities, for your engagement, and for your eagerness to grow.

One of the most confident people I know happens to be my spousal unit, Cindy. After nearly 25 years of marriage, I've grown accustomed to working alongside her in many endeavors. From raising two boys, starting businesses, running schools, planning vacations, and navigating unchartered waters together, I've watched with amazement how she takes on challenge after challenge with boldness and confidence. From the simplest efforts of planning our multi-week road trips, to parenting and daunting business challenges, we make a pretty good team.

Often our endeavors challenge us with vast oceans of unknowns and uncertainties. We thrive on such challenges. As a resourceful and smart woman, Cindy exudes the character trait of confidence to take on and succeed in the challenge at hand.

One day not long ago, we were in a meeting together and were handed some seriously bad news. Cindy had listened to the lead-up conversation and gathered the requisite knowledge to frame a thoughtful yet confident response. The next words out of her mouth would forever alter the course of much of her work. Now, most people in this situation probably would have reacted angrily, and perhaps even stormed out of the room, forever damaging vital relationships. Not Cindy! Due to her experience and confidence, she elegantly and swiftly crafted an excellent resolution to the challenge before us. It ended in a fantastic outcome, and all of us breathed a sigh of relief. I happen to believe she was being interviewed and tested. Bet she didn't expect that.

Adaptivity

One of the students who exhibited such focus and engagement at my talk at Anderson University is named Emily. She also exhibits another much sought-after trait: adaptiveness. She's equipped with a degree in computer science, and we were eager to hire her at Bitwise. Emily also holds a degree in dance and enjoys working with people. After one brief encounter, anyone would recognize Emily as a natural leader. Disney recruited her for an internship – twice! Those rascals beat me to her. While she used neither her computer science nor dance degrees at Disney, she most definitely leveraged her character traits of adaptability and curiosity in her role. She isn't content being a programmer just because of her degree. Rather, she's open-minded to adapt – a character trait that will serve her well.

As they say, change is the only constant. In any field or industry, things are perpetually shifting, and you have to be able to keep up and fill in when and where it's needed. It's a struggle to work with those who are so stuck in their ways that they don't try to expand their knowledge and skills base – those who say, "This is all I know how to do," and refuse to grow. The most useful employee is the one who is capable of filling more than one role, the player who's able and willing to serve the team by playing safety or middle linebacker or lineman.

One of the most adaptive and resourceful individuals with whom I have had the pleasure to work is Rebecca. Rebecca has demonstrated adaptivity year in and year out by taking on tasks, projects, and roles for which she had neither prior experience nor formal training. I've watched her step up while others shirked, dive in while others fled for the doors, lead while others watched…all the time knowing she was sailing into new waters. I recognized the need to fill a somewhat "fuzzy" role just a few months after starting Apprentice University. The role and its corresponding responsibilities were anything but well-defined, but I knew for certain Rebecca was the right person for the job. I had watched her "never back down from a challenge" mindset time and time again, so hiring her was a no-brainer. I'm very certain she didn't expect that!

Curiosity

Adaptiveness is a result of another key character trait: curiosity. When I'm interviewing someone, I'll often ask them to name the last book they read, as this shows me whether or not they desire to seek new knowledge. Expanding your horizons by reading, taking online classes or workshops, and talking to others about their different fields and projects with interest and attentiveness demonstrates a continual desire to learn and grow, and that's the kind of person that is needed in the workforce, in government, in education – in anything. There should never be a time when you say, "I'm going to stop learning for a while." Be a perpetual learner.

My dear friend Wil Davis – co-founder and CEO of Ontario Systems and the one who shared that excellent quote about integrity – also has a lot to say about the concept of curiosity. He issues a challenge to seek to constantly improve oneself, saying, "Are you any good at what you do? You say you're a programmer – are you good at it? You say you're a salesman – are you any good at it? You say you're an accountant – are you getting better? Do you have the same skills you graduated with from college twelve years ago? That's not very good. Your engine is going to run out of fuel."

Are you trying to intake more knowledge and train yourself in new skill sets? Are you continuously curious? Keep moving. Strive for creativity. Demonstrate a propensity to continue to learn. Show interest in a variety of fields, not only because it makes you more useful, but also because it makes life more interesting!

Curiosity can be a strong motivator. I recently had an opportunity to mentor Paige, one of the most curious young adults I have encountered. Paige is a bright, recent high school graduate with an insatiable appetite for learning. She is well read, an incredible writer and very creative. I first encountered Paige through a marketing video she created for Apprentice University. She demonstrated her ability to be intentionally extraordinary by providing this video without being asked. It was truly a work of art!

As a seasoned Talent Spotter, I immediately recognized the marketability and professionalism of her work, so I encouraged and assisted her in starting her own business. Not many teenagers possess the rigor needed to launch their own business, but Paige's curiosity about how business works, including writing contracts, negotiating, and other aspects, enabled her to jump start her business in a matter of weeks. That inherent curiosity was the catalyst that gave her the self-motivation to hang out her shingle. Of course, the money was nice too, but it was not Paige's primary motivator.

Resourcefulness

Growing up, I enjoyed America's pre-Facebook favorite pastime – baseball. I loved to play. Scratch that…I loved to play a *lot* of baseball. There was no position on the field I couldn't, and wouldn't play, but I preferred the positions where I could use my God-given gift of an accurate and reasonably strong throwing arm. My favorite position was pitcher, but I was equally excited to catch or play third base.

I recall one particular game where I was pitching. I was on a Babe Ruth League all-star travel team from my hometown of Frankfort, Indiana. We were really, really good. We were playing an arrogant and well-groomed team from LaPorte, Indiana. (In hindsight, I now believe they bred Jareds to play on their team.) We were winning the game handily and I was pitching a pretty good game when suddenly a fast ball was tipped by the batter, striking my catcher on his unprotected shoulder. He was down for the count, out of the game with a pretty serious injury.

After a very long time-out and helping my friend off the field, our coach looked at me and said, "Suit up, you're catching." Remember, I loved pitching and I was throwing a great game. Slightly disappointed, I swapped my mitt for the catching gear and took over for my injured buddy. I was accustomed to playing the position of catcher and had done it many times before, but… coach, I was winning the game!

As in baseball, being resourceful is crucial in any career. If, for example, you can only play first base, you greatly limit your coach's ability to keep you on the field. Like any career, if you're only good at one thing, you're likely to encounter limitations. Resourcefulness is a character trait which can be developed and is a byproduct of a learning disposition (described in detail earlier in this chapter). They are inseparable character traits.

Talent Spotters readily recognize resourcefulness in an individual. A few years ago I had the opportunity to work closely with a few high school students and provide a grade to them on a final project for school. I coached them through the startup ideas for their project. Throughout the course of my involvement with them, I watched closely how they would play off one another's strengths and weaknesses. Their project was unique and required a stretch for their young imaginations and the questions they were solving were not readily evident. One student, Rachael, stood out because of her adaptability and resourcefulness.

Rachael demonstrated these character traits by drawing upon her previous, albeit brief, work experiences to attempt to solve problems. I could see her wheels spinning as she thought through possible solutions and a variety of ways she could advance their cause. When Rachael didn't have the answer to a given question, she was quick to draw upon her network of friends and their parents for advice. Ultimately, Rachael learned much more than just the answers to the questions she and her team were solving: she learned the art of finding, or inventing, the solution. For those readers old enough to remember the television series *MacGyver*, he would be the poster boy for resourcefulness.

The outcome of the project was well-done, and the richness of the journey of getting there was evident in Rachael's experience. If they had been a baseball team, I'm sure Rachael could have played multiple positions. While important, her grade wasn't nearly as important to me as was developing her skills in resourcefulness, adaptability, and problem solving.

Self-Disciplined and Organized

If you want to make a strong first impression, show up, and show up prepared. Demonstrate self-discipline and make it apparent by turning in assignments on time and by responding to emails promptly (as in several times a day). Train yourself to be organized and prepared by taking notes during an interview or meeting and by arriving on time. If you say you'll be somewhere at a specific time, be there by that time. If you're late once to an event or meeting, it's usually forgiven; if you do it twice, it's noted by your co-workers; if you do it three times…well, three strikes and you're out. Now, things happen and calendars can become quite hectic, but as often as possible, demonstrate respect for others by being punctual.

Self-discipline and organization demonstrate initiative and trustworthiness. If you're known to be the type of person who is always prepared, who can always be counted on to do what you're supposed to do, then you'll be trusted with more. When employers consider whether you're someone they want to hire, little indicators about punctuality and preparedness speak volumes. A strong showing in these areas reflects deeper self-discipline and organization.

Self-Awareness

Once, a young man named Elliott wandered into Bitwise's offices looking a little lost, so I went out to greet him. Elliott was wearing basketball shorts and a t-shirt. His tennis shoes were unlaced, his hair was tousled, and he carried a rolled-up piece of paper in his hand. My first thought was that he was the delivery guy from a local sandwich shop – until I remembered those guys are better groomed and dressed than this person. I then assumed he was just lost and in the wrong office, so I asked if I could help him. He responded by shaking my hand, giving me the rolled-up piece of paper – his resume – and saying, "I'm here for my interview."

I was a bit baffled by this, which he surely guessed by my raised eyebrows. He proceeded to say that he had a meeting with "Scott," inappropriately referring to my business partner Scott Workman by his

21

first name instead of "Mr. Workman," whom he had never previously met. Still confounded and surveying his attire, I asked him if this meeting was scheduled a half hour ago. Nope, it had been booked for a week. I followed up by asking if his car had broken down or some similar situation had arisen to prevent him from dressing properly for the meeting. Nope, he had just figured that the basketball shorts were okay because this was a technology firm. Not wanting to go zero for three, I didn't even bother asking about his hair.

I told this young man that he indeed would not be interviewing with Mr. Workman, that he would not be hired by this firm, and that he should beeline to the local bookstore and buy a book on interviewing. Not only did he display a lack of preparedness and self-discipline, but this man showed absolutely no self-awareness. He didn't realize that what he was doing and what he looked like was completely unacceptable.

Self-awareness is key. Employers don't want to hire someone who doesn't "get it" and isn't responsive to social standards. Demonstrate an awareness of your behavior, of the situation, of what is appropriate and what is not, and act accordingly. And for goodness' sake, dress appropriately for the occasion!

Lack of Drama and Gossip

Few things will overdraw your relational capital account faster than evidence of drama and gossip. Many years ago we were interviewing a young lady named Natalie for a position at our firm. Several of our staff had made her acquaintance prior to the interview. After a rather successful interview, one which left me excited to advance to the next stage of consideration, a member of our team pulled me aside. She had fear written all over her face. It turns out she and Natalie had both played on the same rec-league softball team and Natalie had quite a reputation for causing drama, fabricating stories, and gossiping about her teammates. We'll not recount the drama stories here as they are welcome neither in the workplace nor in this book!

I'm certain Natalie never imagined her behavior with her softball team would abruptly end a career opportunity. She didn't expect it. Her extracurricular behavior sure wasn't going to spill into our culture, spewing highly toxic drama and gossip. Once they take root, drama and gossip are cancerous, and they can take years to eradicate. Such a fatal tumor was not going to grow on my dime.

Weeks after we had told Natalie "no thanks," I spoke to the employee who had pulled me aside. I thanked her for her candidness and willingness to confide in me about Natalie's character. Unlike Natalie, she despised gossip and drama and wanted no part of it. She averted what would inevitably have been a mess. We never spoke of Natalie again, as that itself would be gossip. The relational capital built between our employee and me over this situation didn't go unnoticed. Shortly after the dust settled on this interview, she received a nice promotion, pay increase, and took on more responsibility. I'm certain she didn't expect that.

Sadly, drama is part of the workplace. Drama often manifests itself in the form of gossip. False, or half-truth statements made about someone suddenly become the focus of the day instead of the work at hand. Minor issues get blown out of proportion and people become too sensitive. Sometimes drama and gossip take root when someone shares their personal matters at work. I'm all for healthy, productive, personal relationships in the workplace. They build teamwork, camaraderie, and loyalty amongst the staff, but put your personal matters through a reasonableness test. If they aren't edifying, confidence-building, teamwork-enhancing conversations, move on.

Attitude

I've been around and worked with many students over the years, and one thing that I've noticed is how they acknowledge adults in the room. A shocking number of young people don't bother to say hello or make eye contact when adults enter a room – even if they are adults the kids have known for years. That sounds pretty negative, and it is, but here's the flip side: Because so many students *don't* acknowledge adults and exhibit a positive, respectful attitude, you'll stand out if you do. If there's an adult in the room, smile, say hello, and greet them by name. Acknowledge their presence. Whether you do or don't is noticed.

Attitude is exuded not just by the words you say, but by the way you carry yourself. It's in your body language, whether that is eye rolls or eye contact, scoffing or nodding with engagement. A lack of eye contact often translates the perception that you think you're too good for the other person, and the message you're sending is, "Get away."

Instead, make yourself approachable. Smile, make eye contact, take a second to devote some attention to those around you. This goes back to the quote I mentioned earlier about people not remembering what you did but how you made them feel. If you exude an attitude that says that you're fully present, that you consider all people worth talking to, and that you have time for others, people will remember you.

I frequently have the opportunity to cross paths with many remarkable high school students. Two classmates in particular, Brock and Sutherlin, stand out as having very positive attitudes and consistently demonstrating respect for adults. They're both very bright high school students with outstanding character traits and incredibly rich futures. My wife, Cindy, and I often host events such as movie nights or trips to the local amusement park, and Brock and Sutherlin frequent both. Without failure, both of these students *always* wear a smile and approach the adults responsible for the events to thank them for their preparatory work. Now, of all the students I've had the opportunity to engage with over the years, why would I single out these two? Because they embody intentionally extraordinary behavior in their positive attitude and how it conveys respect for adults. I'm pretty sure they were unaware they were being interviewed.

Supportive

I'm always looking to hire people with a technology background and I have conducted more than my share of interviews with IT professionals. For whatever reason, many IT departments in companies have a reputation of being controlling rather than supportive. I believe this stems from the fact that nearly all our jobs rely upon IT to function and too often the power created from this dependency goes to their head. Okay, I'll step down from my soapbox now...

You've had this happen – suddenly, one day you can't print. (This book isn't long enough for me to share my absolute disdain for printers... but I digress.) You have a huge presentation in just a few minutes and the blasted thing is just blinking. You're stuck. In a panic, you shoot a quick email to the IT help desk who promptly responds with an email stating you're "in the queue." Now, you have no idea whether the queue is one minute or one week long, so you write back, pleading your case to expedite the help. In return, you receive an email that states, "We all have deadlines. You should have planned better." Sigh...

I often ask about scenarios like these during an interview, trying to discern whether a candidate stepped up to support a distressed co-worker or played the control card and left them to suffer. My goal is to determine if the candidate has a supportive or controlling demeanor that may translate to a difficult employee.

A good friend of mine has a very successful business. He asked me whether he should hire a person to help manage his company's technology needs or outsource the role to a local firm. We discussed and decided it was best he hire someone as his needs were significant and increasing. He had several candidates and asked if I would participate in the interviews with the best three to select the right candidate. Of course, I agreed to help my friend. We established hiring criteria, salary expectations, benefits, etc. This position paid well - it was a good job.

One of the finalists was named Tom. Ironically, I knew Tom and had interacted with him a bit, as his employer at the time was a client of my firm. In this relationship, we worked mostly with the marketing staff at this company and minimally with their IT team, but oh, I remembered Tom. Unfortunately, it's all too common in the business world that marketing and IT departments don't play well together. I was privy to and saw firsthand the unnecessary delays placed upon our project by Tom. Our project was time sensitive and the marketing staff was under a lot of pressure. Like the printer scenario, IT wasn't helpful. They took forever to respond to simple questions, didn't show up for critical meetings, created unnecessary delays, and put pressure on the whole team.

Tom wasn't hired and shortly thereafter left our client's company, which is probably a good thing. Imagine the look on Tom's face when he saw me sitting across the interview table. He wasn't expecting that!

Not a 59er

In baseball, after hitting the ball, a runner's job is to reach first base before the ball reaches the mitt of the first baseman. Giving it his all and pushing through, the runner may continue past first base, veering right. This is commonly referred to as "sprint by first" in baseball lingo. The runner who gives up pushing himself five paces from first base will certainly watch the rest of the game from the dugout. The coach would surely be questioning the character and resolve of the player if he didn't push hard to the finish.

Likewise, the individual who doesn't give it all by pushing himself on the job to and through "quitting time" is certain to raise eyebrows. I call these individuals 59ers. The name 59er coincides with the time on the clock at which these employees consistently knock-off for the day. Let's assume, for the sake of our story about 59ers, that their work day is approximately 8:00AM - 5:00PM. A 59er, every day, day in and day out, somehow miraculously reaches a logical, practical, and convenient stopping point in their work in order to leave at 4:59 – on the dot. By 5:00, their chair is cold and they're long gone. Let's call that last "minute" a rounding error, but that's not the point. The point is that sometime well before 4:59, they start "packing up" to head out for the day, leaving 10-15 minutes each day as their "rounding error."

> *A 59er, every day, day in and day out, somehow miraculously reaches a logical, practical, and convenient stopping point in their work in order to leave at 4:59 – on the dot.*

Remember, even though 59ers have a job, they're always being observed by their employer, looking for opportunities for advancement, grooming, improvement. I often wonder if 59ers are aware of the message, albeit passively, they are sending to their employer. Like the base runner in baseball, the employee who packs up early *every single day* is telling their employer they're a clock watcher and are unwilling to push hard and excel to the end (sprint by first base). This is not a becoming character trait in an employee and Talent Spotters do take notice of these things.

A former employee, Brett, was a pretty sharp young man who was as punctual as you might imagine. He had a professional role and a salary exempt (we'll explore this term more shortly) position. Like clockwork, he'd arrive each day to work at the same time. Like a conductor who managed the timing of trains in days of old, you could set your watch by his exit time at 4:59 every day. Atomic clocks could only hope to be so punctual! Each day, Brett could be seen pulling out of the parking lot at exactly 5:00 PM. In other words, Brett never sprinted by first base. This went on for a while and I had a good opportunity to ask Brett why he was so adamant about being out the door at 4:59 – a 59er. He simply stated, "It's quitting time, right?" I didn't press the issue, but I noted it for a subsequent, more timely conversation. His response led me to believe he wasn't aware of the message he was sending. Nobody ever bothered to train him that 59ers end up watching the game from the dugout. I attempted to have conversations with Brett about his 59er addiction, but it was simply a foreign concept to him.

Now, Brett may not have realized the message he was sending, but in the back of my mind his 59er behavior demonstrated an absence of commitment, dedication, and work ethic. Non-59ers realize that, in professional positions, some days start earlier than others and some days run longer than others. That's the whole pretense of a professional – especially one who is *salary exempt.* Let's briefly explore the term salary exempt. A salaried position means you're paid the same amount each pay period rather than an hourly rate. You're expected to work a baseline number of hours for that salary. An individual in a salaried *exempt* position is not eligible for, or is exempt from, overtime pay. Most employees in creative or technical roles are usually salary exempt employees. Most salary exempt employers expect a little give and take – arrive a little early one day, leave a little early the next. If you fly to a meeting in another city, you arrive a little later in the morning after your return – a balance. Being salary exempt does *not* mean you're exempt from working after 5:00.

> *Being salary exempt does not mean you're exempt from working after 5:00.*

When it came time to consider promotions, bonuses, pay increases, and the like, Brett's supervisor had already noted in his file that he was a 59er. "Brett demonstrates an absence of commitment and dedication necessary to support our team. Our meetings must always end by precisely 4:55, even if we're not finished." Try as we might to change this frustrating behavior, we were not successful. Brett was never promoted in large part due to his perceived lack of passion for his work and absence of a teamwork mindset. He didn't work for us much longer after my chat with him about his 59er behavior.

Grit

Grit is a great word and a highly desirable character trait sought by Talent Spotters. Individuals with grit demonstrate passion and perseverance. Angela Lee Duckworth gave a wonderful TED Talk[2] on grit. She shared that the grittiest students in her classes weren't the smartest nor did they come from a wealthy background. Rather, they demonstrated a relentless pursuit and stamina to complete their work, and were therefore more likely to graduate.

To inculcate and instill grit, our students at Apprentice University spend the first three weeks with us working at a pig farm. At "the farm", as it is affectionately called, our students are part of the team – a team whose day starts at 6:29:59 each day and ends around 4pm. 59ers will quickly find themselves doing some seriously nasty work at the farm. The work day includes every task imaginable and required in confinement pig farming. It's hot, stinky, and physically demanding work. Things move quickly at the farm. It's big, busy, and ever-changing. We hope the grit inculcated in our students teaches them how to persevere through tough jobs and to accomplish such tasks with excellence. We also want our students to understand the importance of rigor – an unwavering dedication to see a task to completion. Few things are more exciting to Talent Spotters than identifying an individual with strong measures of rigor, perseverance, and grit.

Remember my friend Mike Alley, who places high import on integrity and character when determining with whom he engages? He credits the growth of Fifth Third Bank in Central Indiana to the grit of his team, saying:

> "A classic story of perseverance and having the right attitude would be our entry into this market. At Fifth Third in '89, we were really at the frontier entering the market, and the key to our success was having a team that was totally committed to one another, a team that didn't know that they weren't supposed to be successful at this. We just had hard drive and a commitment to get

---

[2] https://www.ted.com/talks/angela_lee_duckworth_grit_the_power_of_passion_and_perseverance

it done, and as a result, we went from a $45 million asset bank to over half a billion, on our own pure growth, with no acquisitions at all, in just a few years, which is pretty amazing. But it was the team – it was having that group of people that was willing to work hard and make sacrifices for one another."

Grit is frequently demonstrated by someone on the hunt for employment. Looking for a job, especially as a teenager, is a tough task. With minimal demonstrable skills and a rather skinny resume, most teens find looking for a job a rather frustrating endeavor. Those young job seekers with grit, rigor, and perseverance are far more likely to land a job than their peers without such attributes. Just think about it for a minute: positive is to negative as north is to south; grit is to determination as slothfulness is to laziness. Over time, Talent Spotters develop a keen eye for talent with grit as they know those individuals have the resilience and determination to complete the job at hand.

> *Those young job seekers with grit, rigor, and perseverance are far more likely to land a job than their peers without such attributes.*

Hudson is one of the most determined young men I know. He is the youngest of my two boys. Hudson demonstrated motivation and grit while searching for a part-time job a couple years ago. He asked for a little help in preparing his resume, but after that he was determined to find a job on his own. "Dad, I'm going to do this on my own," he told me after I offered to help make some introductions. He researched job openings in the area day in and day out. Relentlessly, wearing a nice shirt with a collar and khaki pants, he'd march into stores, resume in hand, determined to place it and his application in the hands of the manager. He did it the old-fashioned way! As you might imagine, meeting the manager in person was rare, but that didn't stop Hudson. For weeks he'd research new opportunities, suit up, print a new resume, and march in asking to hand his paperwork to the manager. Hudson demonstrated determination, grit, and resilience in the face of many dead ends. Sadly, most businesses just ignored his intentionally-prepared application and resume, choosing to not respond at all to his query for employment. (I find this behavior on behalf of employers rude, but that's a subject for another book and another day.)

Hudson's perseverance paid off. He landed a great starter job at the local coffee shop at just 16 years old and has subsequently advanced through the ranks to the role of a shift manager. There aren't many people who can get out of bed at 4:45am to be at work by 5:30, especially teenagers. Not that he enjoys such an early start time, but each day he arrives at work early in the morning, on time and ready to work. He is contributing to his relational capital account with his boss and co-workers by supporting his teammates with his reliability. For certain, Hudson likes receiving a paycheck, but I know he wants to please his customers and to continue to improve his opportunities with his employer. As you might imagine, I like telling Hudson's story of perseverance and grit. Good job, Hud.

So ... Now What?

You are now familiar with the numerous characteristics which, combined, will leave a powerful first – and lasting – positive impression. But where do you go from here? How do you develop your character? How do you recognize gaps in these traits in your life, and what do you do about it?

First, remember that you ARE the company you keep. If you hang out with slugs, you'll be a slug. If you seek to grow and improve yourself, then associate yourself with friends and mentors who exhibit the same desire for strong character and who exemplify the traits you wish to develop.

After doing that, complete a thorough self-analysis. Perhaps, as you read this chapter, you recognized one or two traits you feel that you embody well, as well as a few that you realize you may not demonstrate very often. Write those down, and explain why you either do or do not exhibit those traits. Create specific exercises for yourself to grow in the areas that need improvement.

Sometimes, however, we simply can't perform an unbiased analysis of ourselves, and it's usually significantly easier to improve when you have someone pushing and helping us along the way. This is why I encourage you to find a few trusted friends, mentors, teachers, and/ or parents who can tactfully but objectively help you identify your strengths and weaknesses and provide you challenges through which they can supportively guide you.

This exercise of self-analysis and looking to others for guidance in your own path of improvement is crucial in any area of life. It demonstrates a truly teachable spirit! I find it so important, in fact, that I designed an exercise based upon this method and wrote it in the curriculum for the college-aged students of Apprentice University, an experience-based learning program that I founded. Remember: a highly sought-after person of strong character is marked by a continual willingness to grow and expand – a perpetual learning disposition!

Applying This Chapter

Here is a useful exercise I encourage many young professionals to undertake. It may help you better understand your strengths and weaknesses. You might recognize this exercise as a "360-degree review."

1. Visit the Career Education/Preparation page of Columbia University (found at time of writing at http://www.careereducation.columbia. edu/resources/tipsheets/skills-business-etiquette), or something similar.

2. Take some time to reflect upon, write down, and elaborate on the following:

    - Key elements you learned from the workplace etiquette checklist.
    - The areas in which *you know* you can improve relative to workplace and social etiquette.

3. Conduct three types of interviews:

    - Three close, adult, family members
    - Two peers (friends, classmates, similarly-aged co-workers, etc.)
    - One or two mentors or teachers

4. For every person you interview, ask them to review the list on the Columbia University website and the list of character traits in this chapter, keeping in mind they are using these lists as a yardstick to measure you. Ask them to be completely honest and candid with you, as they elaborate upon three to five personal character traits, behaviors, or habits you have which:

- Challenge you professionally (currently or in the future) that are inconsistent with this checklist (in other words, things you need to work on)
- Demonstrate exceptionalism, excellence, and strengths

5. Record and journal the responses of your interviewees without editing (verbatim). You're after the most candid feedback possible.

6. Rank and discuss your perceived difficulty in addressing each of the weaknesses referenced by each interviewee. Conversely, discuss how you will continue to excel and maintain humility in addressing the items in which you are perceived to possess exceptionalism and excellence.

7. Prepare a detailed timeline and action plan for addressing any of the weaknesses. Don't be afraid to ask your interviewees for help in this step – they likely have good ideas.

8. Follow up! Review these lists with your interviewees to see how you're improving and what you might do better. This step will provide invaluable feedback and it's a good exercise in humility.

CHAPTER TWO

PERSONAL BRAND

PERSONAL BRAND

Who are you? What do you want to be remembered by and associated with? When people think of you, what do you want to come to their mind?

This is your personal brand — a term that I find rather cheesy and overused, but the importance of its meaning can't be overlooked. How can you define and market your personal brand?

I recently had a conversation with my friend, Dr. Erin Albert. (You'll get to meet her a little later.) While discussing personal branding, she immediately commented on how important it is to *know yourself* before you try to define your brand for others. What are you passionate about? What makes you tick? What motivates you? What do you know best? How do you stand out from others? Your personal brand comes from the answers to those questions.

Once you answer those questions, it's up to you to protect, grow, and make known your brand. How do you do that? That's what we'll be discussing in this chapter. Let's explore some elements and representations of your personal brand.

Resume

I have read thousands of resumes and it is readily obvious who devotes time to diligently prepare this condensed representation of themselves. There are countless books on resume writing. If you are going to buy a book on resume writing, make sure the author has experience in hiring people from resumes, not just in the academic exercise of writing. Filter the counsel of an advice-giver on resume writing when that person has little or no experience in the role of a Talent Spotter.

> *If you are going to buy a book on resume writing, make sure the author has experience in hiring people from resumes, not just in the academic exercise of writing.*

I was recently discussing resumes with a group of college-age students. They asked the common questions about how many pages it should be, how to format the resume, what size font to use, if it should be in color, etc. The general formatting, font size, structure, etc., of your resume is mostly irrelevant. Of course, it must be concise and should certainly demonstrate a progression of complexity in your work experience. They had learned to limit their resume to one page, to make it all about the facts, to eliminate anything considered personal, and that there was but one appropriate format. As expected, their advisor had never used a resume for hiring.

I consider myself an experienced Talent Spotter and a quick study on translating resumes which lead to interviews and hires. Experience counts. It is through this lens of experience that we will explore the subject of resumes. The bottom line goal of a resume is this: you are seeking to capture the attention of a Talent Spotter by describing your personal brand. How you accomplish this goal should be unique and individualized, matching your personal brand, not some vanilla, generic package. What does that look like?

First, there is no law or rule on page count. The one-page rule is bologna. If it takes you a few pages to describe your personal brand and to tell your story, that's great. Talent Spotters want to know who you are, your character, motivators, strengths, weaknesses, passions, goals, and values. About now, my human resource professional friends are undoubtedly cringing, shaking their head, and yelling, "No, no, no! You can't describe values in a resume." In the politically-correct, heightened-sensitivity, lawsuit-primed culture we're in today, employers have to be cautious about handling your resume and your interview. Unfortunately, this makes the challenge of sharing your personal brand very difficult.

I prefer resumes that cautiously balance character, experience, and learning, first telling me about character, followed by the individual's story of experience and learning (remember the "learning cycle"?) over the course of a few pages. The degree to which you can tell your story depends on the intended receiver. Larger corporations prefer the more traditional, less personal resumes whereas smaller firms tend to be more relaxed. How in the world do you navigate that balance?

But here's the trick: You.com (more on this later). Spend some time preparing a little personal website about you and place a link at the bottom of your resume. This approach gives you a chance to share your personal brand in a way that accurately reflects you. I know, once again, my human resource friends are shaking their heads and yelling "No!", but as a Talent Spotter, I want to know you and what makes you tick. I want to understand how you, added to my teams, are going to add value, impact our culture, and improve our organization. It's extremely difficult to obtain this information from a vanilla resume and asking many questions of a personal nature in an interview is illegal. This quandary puts the employer in a real pickle. The bottom line is this: know your recipient. People hire people they like, trust, and with whom they connect. If your resume doesn't accurately reflect your personal brand, it makes it more difficult for a Talent Spotter to glean who you truly are.

We live in a multimedia, color-rich world with an ever-expanding number of clever ways to connect with one another. To keep the Talent Spotter's attention, your resume should stand out. Gone are the days of boring black and white resumes. Thank goodness! Now, we have tools to create captivatingly colorful resumes such as Visual CV.[3] Just remember – this doesn't mean the contents of your resume can be sloppy. A pretty resume written poorly is like lipstick on a pig. It might make the pig a little more presentable, but it's still a pig. Likewise, a well-packaged resume must also be well-written.

> *A pretty resume written poorly is like lipstick on a pig. It might make the pig a little more presentable, but it's still a pig.*

A bit later in this book, you'll get to meet Charlotte and my good friend Joseph. I hope their story will emphasize the importance of your resume accurately reflecting your work history and experiences. This book would be thousands of pages long if I told all the stories of fiction-filled resumes I have reviewed. Rest assured, prospective employers will check the references you provide, and the statements and claims you make on your resume. As my mom, Deana, taught me, "Honesty is the best policy." A personal brand associated with deception is irrecoverable.

Recently, I received a resume from a young lady named Allison, whom I did not previously know. Her resume contents were impressive, clearly demonstrating her outstanding academic achievements and extracurricular activities. She had nominal work experience, but such is to be expected of a student. It was well-written and sufficiently descriptive as to give me a snapshot of her character. I was quite impressed.

More impressive than her resume was the cover letter she included in her email. In that letter, she demonstrated her thorough research on Bitwise. Her cover letter very succinctly asked for an interview and she included dates and times she would be available over the following few weeks. Within a few days of receiving her resume, I received three

---

[3] https://www.visualcv.com

40

letters of recommendation from her references, all specifically written to me and referencing the position she desired to have with our firm. This is important: There was no published position for which she was applying, but her thorough research provided her with confidence that she possessed the talents and skills necessary to be an asset to our firm.

As you might imagine, I scheduled the interview with Allison. I complimented her on the research she had conducted and the approach she had taken to secure an interview. Admittedly, going into the interview, I was a bit timid given the preparations and thoroughness of this young lady. Stepping into the meeting room, I was greeted by a well-dressed, well-prepared candidate. As always, I ask interviewees if they have any preliminary questions about our firm, specifics about a given role, or other such things, before I start asking questions. I like this approach as it gives the candidate a chance to minimize any doubts or uncertainties they might have. I wasn't prepared for what transpired next!

I've conducted hundreds and hundreds of interviews over the years, but none like this one. Allison took the opportunity to ask several questions. I was being grilled. Grilled on the character, culture, and values, of our firm. She asked specific questions about my involvement in the position she was seeking, the background of the others with whom she might be working and their experience level. Gulp...grilled indeed. Allison proceeded to tell me that she loved hearing my stories during the class and decided she was going to work for Bitwise. Her questioning of me lasted about forty minutes, and then she asked if I had questions for her.

Never before had I experienced such an incredible interview. Allison's preparedness and assertiveness left me awestruck. At the conclusion of our interview, which lasted about 90 minutes, Allison told me she had been researching Bitwise since the day she learned I was speaking to her class. She had studied my background and bio, and was convinced we were her next place of employment. Little did I know, I was the one being interviewed during our time together and she was selecting Bitwise for her next position. I didn't expect that!

Allison was hired for the position she was seeking.

On the flip side of the Allison story is the resume and cover letter I received from Jaclyn. In this case, there were very specific application instructions and a succinct job description for an open position. In Jaclyn's cover letter, she misspelled my last name (a common occurrence) and the greeting was not, "Dear Mr. Brumbarger," but rather, "Hey." Jaclyn was seeking a position with Apprentice University. Her letter read: "Apprentice University is a very hands on. There is more potential in this school than you know. I will make your school work. Having no debt means you can buy things." You just can't make these things up...is your head shaking now?

Jaclyn received a very polite "thank you" rejection email. Period.

Publishing

Demonstrating your ability to synthesize information, formulate an opinion, articulate your thoughts, and substantiate your position with supporting evidence is an art and a critical element of your personal brand. Few things help a Talent Spotter gain an insight into one's character, values, and perspectives better than published material. For example, in this book, you're gaining insight into what I value and look for when seeking new talent. Writing and publishing enables others to accurately appreciate and understand you, your character, and your personal brand. Admittedly, it can be a rather unnerving challenge to be authentic and transparent in your writing (this book has been for me), but well-written prose is insightful.

Publishing does not necessarily mean writing a book, but actually assumes many forms. Several years ago, my son Tanner developed a website on politics. The purpose of the website was to encourage older teens to become more thoughtfully aware of and engaged in politics. It began as a simple blog, but quickly grew into a very popular website for youth people interested in politics. Tanner recruited several close friends and classmates, including my editor for this book, Isabella, to contribute to his website. It wasn't long until nationally syndicated outlets were picking up his articles. Tanner's contact list immediately expanded to include some national big wigs and hootie-tooties in the political world. Tanner, a whopping sixteen years old at the time, accepted invitations to speak at national conferences. He and Isabella earned press credentials at a conference in Washington, DC. What did Tanner's writing have to do with his personal brand? He built name recognition and a small relational capital account balance with some very significant names in the political world. At sixteen years old, Tanner demonstrated that it's never too early to start building your personal brand. Tanner sure made his dad proud!

I have a good friend, Dr. Erin Albert. Erin is quite accomplished. In addition to being an author, Erin earned a PharmD, MBA, JD, and altMBA. Erin has created for herself one of the most respected personal brands of anyone I know. Through hard work, publishing, and prolific and insightful writing, she has carved out a niche for herself as an entrepreneur, thinker, and writer. She is often called upon as a keynote speaker and frequently appears on the local business television shows as a guest speaker. I had the opportunity to discuss with Erin how publishing has assisted her career.

"When I started my first book back in 2007, I never intended for it to be a book. It was something that was going to be published in a peer reviewed journal," she said. Erin, who worked as a medical science liaison in the pharmaceutical industry at the time, loved her job and was interested in studying the whole industry in pharmaceuticals of medical liaisons, such as job satisfaction and the different structures within different companies. After gathering five years' worth of data and submitting it to a journal, she was frustrated when, six months later, they still hadn't let her know when it would be published. So, she pulled the manuscript and published a book instead.

"That was my first business card, because books are really about business," she said. "That was the first book in the field on medical science liaisons. Now there are subsequently other books published, but being the author of the first book in the space, I chaired national meetings on medical liaisons and medical communications. I presented offshoots of some of the data in other venues and presentations on some of the data within the book itself. So [writing and publishing] can turn into speaking engagements and brand awareness."

From there, Erin learned to love writing and publishing, aiming to publish at least one new book every year. "For me," she said, "it's almost like a journey of learning about something new, and I want to take people along with me."

Through writing and publishing, not only do you learn and grow, but Erin's right – you create new "business cards." You mark yourself as an expert and resource in your field, and your writing is evidence of your authority, experience, and brand.

Blogging is another excellent way to promote and manage your personal brand. Consistently sharing your thoughts on a particular theme of topics over a short time will propel your name to the forefront of people's minds when it comes to that subject. Bloggers are much like the columnists of the newspaper era, but without the editorial filtering and dimensionally-constrained elements of yesteryear. Take, for example, Matt Walsh. Matt Walsh is a relative newcomer to the world of news and opinions. You may have read his work. Matt established his personal brand blogging a few years ago and now you can find his work online through many serious news sources. When I first discovered Matt, his work was mainly focused on education and has subsequently expanded to address a much broader range of subjects.

Tanner, Isabella, Erin, and Matt all improved their personal brands through writing and publishing, but such is not always the case. Earlier this year, I needed some assistance preparing a research paper. As always, I had neither enough time nor people to tackle this project. After a little searching, I found Kelly, a professional writer with experience doing similar work to that which we needed. Time was of the essence, so Kelly and I scheduled to meet right away. In the interim, she forwarded some of her previous work to review and to help size up whether she was the right fit for the job. Her work product was astounding. I was eager to meet Kelly and get our project started immediately. The morning of our meeting, I came across a blog she had recently posted that caused me to do a double take. Her prior work had been so well done and left such a strong impression of her personal brand that when I discovered this typo-laden, poorly-written post, I had to question the authenticity of her previous work. Ultimately, Kelly wasn't hired for the job after my research turned up yet more poorly-written articles. I'm not sure what she was thinking, but clearly she wasn't expecting me to find her otherwise substandard work.

Speaking

Speaking engagements, like publishing, go a long way in advancing your personal brand. Most people would rather have surgery without anesthesia than stand on a stage and speak in public. It's really not that bad, and becomes easier with practice. Getting started in public speaking does require some preparation and effort. Public speaking and publishing, especially in combination, are quite possibly the two most powerful ways to further your personal brand. Speaking on a subject in which you have experiences consistent with your personal brand is key. Attempting to speak on a subject outside your domain of expertise, regardless of how tempting it may be, is never a good idea.

So, how do you go about getting started in public speaking? There are many helpful books on this topic, so I'll not try to cover all that ground again. I have a simple method I have used in the past to develop speeches. The goal of this approach is to find a subject in which you can passionately demonstrate your interest, but also one consistent with your personal brand.

The first step is to identify some key topics or issues in which you have both experience and passion (think Venn diagram) that correlate with what you want your personal brand to represent. We'll call this your sweet spot. Those topics found in the intersection of your experiences and passions are likely to be items you'll find more rewarding to research, present, and defend. Second, do some homework on the leading-edge thinking on that subject. What are their opinions and views and how might yours differ? Next, think about how your intended audience will receive your ideas and content. Will they find it intriguing, leaving them craving more? Finally, consider how you might position yourself in their league by filtering their positions through your values and personal brand, adding your own position on a given subject. Use caution when selecting topics upon which to speak. It will be brutally and painfully evident you're winging it if you attempt to speak on a topic outside your sweet spot.

I have a talk I give from time to time on "social dexterity." In fact, this book is loosely based upon the outline of that talk. I define social dexterity as "expediting the transition from academics to career." My anticipated audiences are high school and college-age students. I desire that they understand the elements I believe – check that; the elements I *know* – are necessary for them to possess in order to compete in the high-wage, high-demand, knowledge-based careers of a global economy. A tall undertaking! These are the same topics and subjects we wrestle with in our work at Apprentice University, so I am well-versed in the subject matter. I am passionate about producing well-prepared leaders at Apprentice University and continuously improving our students' social dexterity is paramount in achieving this goal. My talk focusing on social dexterity is easy to present, as the content is something about which I'm extraordinarily passionate.

Early in my career, I was invited to speak on a subject about which I knew very little. I was eager to promote our company brand so I accepted the job. At this stage in my career, I had been self-employed for a number of years and was enjoying the fruits of our labor by taking month-long vacations to the desert southwest in our motorhome. We chronicled our trips on our family website. Our friends, co-workers, and business associates enjoyed our daily blogs and photos. A member of a local trade association was tracking our trip and must have thought I knew something about the popular phrase "work-life balance" when he asked me to speak about it. I had him fooled! Not wanting to procrastinate, I started working on my talk several days before I was to speak. It's an easy subject, right? Work – check. Life – check. Balance – okay, I can make that up. How hard could it be anyway? I broke out my trusty process of first finding the intersection of experience and passion. Next, I started researching leading-edge thinkers on this subject. That's when it hit me – I was doomed. Whoa…there were some big thinkers on this subject and they were well-respected in the journals. There was no way in the world I was going to have the knowledge necessary to position myself as an authority on this subject and, of course, I was out of time. As you might imagine, my talk was bland and the audience reviews were negative. Thank goodness they were civil enough not to throw fruit. The moral of this story is there's no faking it when it comes to giving a speech. Stay in your swim lane of experience.

Associations

I can hear it now, all these years later: "If you're walking down the street with a bunch of boys and they start throwing rocks at windows, you leave, or else you're as guilty as they are." – Jack, my dad. That simple life lesson has stuck with me forever and has been useful on many occasions. You have probably heard the phrase "You're only as good as the company you keep." When it comes to degrading your personal brand, few things can damage your reputation faster than associating with the wrong crowd. In the Bible, Paul, quoting the Greek poet

Menander (342 BC – 292 BC), in his first letter to the church in Corinth warned, "Do not be misled: 'Bad company corrupts good character'" (1 Corinthians 15:33). Indeed, much has been written about associating with the right and wrong people.

> "Do not be misled: 'Bad company corrupts good character'" (1 Corinthians 15:33).

Conversely, solid company and associations can improve your personal brand. But, let's be cautious about this. I'm not proposing you flood social media with hundreds of selfies of you with your rich buddies at the country club for the purpose of building your personal brand. I'm not talking about hanging out with the character-void "cool kids" for image improvement. Pass on that, it's not important. For your maturation and subsequently for your personal brand to grow, it's important to think about the company you keep. Consider your own circle of friends and your networks. Are your friends causing you to grow and mature personally, spiritually, intellectually, and professionally? Are you challenging your friends to grow and mature in the same way? I encourage you to push yourself by engaging with people who challenge you to be better. If you're the smartest person in the room, you're in the wrong room.

I grew up in Frankfort, Indiana. In that small town, everybody knows everybody and everybody knows everybody else's business too. I never understood the need for the *Frankfort Times* because by the time the newspaper made it to your doorstep, you had already heard the front page news three times over. Like most little towns, the company you keep is very well known. I went to school with a girl named Darla and our moms were very close friends.

When starting Apprentice University a few years ago, I was looking for a pig farm in Central Indiana to send our students to at the start of their career with us. I wanted to teach grit and the value of hard work, and couldn't think of a better way to do so than by requiring students to work on a pig farm. I quickly learned that not many farmers jump at having college students hang out at their farms learning about hard work. One evening during a talk about Apprentice University, I mentioned that I was looking for a farmer with whom to partner. A few days later I was given the name of my now dear friend Keith Schoettmer. Keith invited me to visit and discuss our burgeoning friendship, an offer I readily accepted. After a brief meeting, we reached a gentleman's agreement, shook hands, and agreed to have our students work on his farm. I was elated. As I was pulling out of the driveway, I heard my name being called from across the farm. It was Keith's wife, Darla. Darla had seen the email request I sent to Keith and told him, "Keith, you've got to do this. I know Ron. We grew up together." The initial deposit into that relational capital account with my friend Darla was made in grade school and although we hadn't seen one another for many years, she remembered the company I kept.

These days we have a relatively new set of challenges regarding the company we keep: social media. Without exception, for every candidate I consider for any position whatsoever, I review their social media friends, posts, tweets, and so on. More than one person has been declined a job offer or admission to college due in large part to their social media friend list. While reviewing your social media accounts, Talent Spotters take into account the company you keep. I'm mindful that this can seem offensive and is not politically correct, but that's okay. This is how the real world works. Here's the deal: if your social media friend group is, metaphorically, throwing rocks through windows, you are at risk of being considered "one of them." Recently, I was discussing this very subject with a group of college students. They were of an opinion that, since their peer group didn't subscribe to the "social media consideration theory," it didn't much matter. It was just old school. I doubt there are many 19-year old Talent Spotters conducting interviews these days. It matters. It matters a lot.

You.com

There are few tools better suited to sharing and promoting your personal brand than a personal website. There are many tools on the market these days for building small, personal websites of decent quality. Like social media, if you share the URL to your personal website, rest assured Talent Spotters will visit. They may have never met you, but either your personal website or social media is likely the way they will form their first opinions about you. Such is unavoidable and, because of this, it had better be pristine.

Like any business website (or houseplant), your personal website will require some periodic care and feeding. If you update your resume for distribution, you must have the same resume on your website. If you're in a career utilizing graphic design or any type of writing, your sample work had better be amazing and current. If you're doing video production, your website should have many video samples of your work. The challenge to using a website as your portfolio is the amount of work you must endure to keep it current. Last year's portfolio or your forgotten resume will tarnish your personal brand. If you are going to commit to a website to showcase your personal brand or work portfolio, you must commit to keeping it current. Keep in mind, however, that once you distribute your resume with your personal website included, you're committed. Your resume may remain in circulation for a long time. It could be placed in a "consider interviewing later" folder in a human resources office only to be pulled out a year later.

We were once preparing to interview a candidate for a sales position at Bitwise. His name was James. A friend had provided his resume, and his work experience and background impressed us. James paid close attention to detail on his resume. It was polished and well written. We sometimes like to ask for references before interviews as it gives us more to explore during the questions and answers of an interview. We checked out the references he provided and they all came back very positive. We had a few days before our interview and I was reviewing our team's preliminary feedback. I decided to do a little Google search on James to see if anything interesting might turn up. Well, apparently James had built a website, or an unreasonable facsimile thereof, to share his personal brand – a brand that appeared to exist before he cleaned up his act. Unfortunately for James, he had long since forgotten about his old website, but it told an interesting story – one he surely didn't want us to discover. Now, I'm all for second, even third chances, but James…what were you thinking?! I wish I had conducted that little search sooner and saved our team some time. Needless to say, we didn't interview James, but we did remind him about his old website.

Extraordinary

Being extraordinary means standing out from the crowd. These days it seems unfashionable, or no longer in vogue, to be extraordinary. We are in an odd place culture-wise where most people, especially our younger adults, would rather blend in than stand out. Perhaps this sentiment arises from peer pressure to conform and be accepted, but to be noticed by a Talent Spotter, you must think and act in extraordinary ways.

What does being extraordinary look like? Remember Allison? Allison was extraordinary in several ways. Her resume and references were extraordinary. Her assertiveness, while controlled, was extraordinary. She dressed in an extraordinary fashion for her interview. She was extraordinary in those areas desirable by Talent Spotters.

However, extraordinary could also be interpreted as extreme or odd. Remember the young man who showed up in his shorts and t-shirt for an interview? He was oddly, even extremely, underdressed for an interview. He was extraordinary, for sure, but in a non-desirable way. How do you know if your "extraordinariness" is desirable or out-of-bounds in the eyes of Talent Spotters? Chances are, if you have to ask this question, it's likely out-of-bounds. For sure, the definition of extraordinary is relative to one's domain or community. Frequently

I see students gauging what's normal versus what's extraordinary based on the dress, actions, and words of their peers. Here's the challenge with this yardstick: your peers or fellow students aren't hiring you!

Recently, I was a guest speaker for a business school event at a local university in Indiana. Prior to my talk, I was the guest of honor at a formal dinner with about a dozen hand-picked students. Each of the students had dressed professionally. They were obviously groomed and prepared for the event, having received training in dining etiquette (more on this later in our book) and professional demeanor. Their handshakes were solid, their smiles genuine, and their eye contact consistent. What a talent-rich environment! It was a little intimidating and was a challenge to identify the leaders from among this group of extraordinary students. They were all quite gifted. Their yardstick for being extraordinary was not one another, but the balance of their peers on campus.

I was curious to see how and if a leader from amongst this group might emerge. Would any of them take me up on my offer to buy lunch or assist in developing their business plans? Would they reach out and ask for introductions for networking? During dinner, I discussed the importance of international travel to help shape young professionals. I discussed some of the trips and groups I had led to South America and Eastern Europe. One young lady, Emily (a different Emily from the first chapter on Character), stepped up and asked to participate in my next trip to South America. Her willingness to hear my advice regarding international travel and promptly act on it was impressive. I was looking for a leader to emerge via a simple request for coffee, not join my next international trip! Her hurdle to be extraordinary given her peer group was quite high, but she found a way to do so. Her decisiveness and leadership characteristics weren't lost on me and her resume remained on my desk for a long time.

Being extraordinary ought to become routine in your way of thinking, behaving, and interacting with others. Being extraordinary doesn't mean, by the way, being flamboyant or outlandish. In fact, any relational capital you might build with another person, whether they're a Talent Spotter or not, is swiftly wasted by flamboyant behavior.

On the other hand, naturally extraordinary people are immediately identifiable in a large crowd by Talent Spotters. Perhaps it's because they have practiced being extraordinary, or they simply stand at the front of the crowd. Either way, for certain, extraordinary talent is challenging to find these days and is most certainly in very high demand.

A few years ago I was helping start a new school. Although it was a second campus of an existing school, the staff, teachers, families, culture, and leadership all had to be developed from the ground up. It was a significant undertaking to be certain. This campus was to inherit the practices, technology, and processes of the original campus, which meant the learning curve was rather steep for everyone involved at the new campus. Our use of technology in this school was significant, to say the least.

After summer passed and the second campus was up and operational, I attended their open house in order to meet some of the new families and students who had enrolled. We were bursting at the seams with new students and families. It was, to say the least, exhilarating and yet intimidating as I questioned how in the world we were going to get this many parents and staff up to speed on all our technology and processes in just a few weeks. What had I done?!

Apparently, I wasn't alone in recognizing this knowledge gap as one of the teachers, Angie, had a similar concern. She anticipated the challenge the staff and parents would face as they worked to become proficient with our tools and technology. Angie took it upon herself, without prompting or request, to create a training video for new parents. As you might imagine, when I first saw this video, I thought, "Well, that's nice, these families won't have to flounder around getting on board." Then, it occurred to me – there was extraordinary talent on the other end of those videos. Who was this person who had identified this need and created these incredible videos, without being asked or paid to do so?

After just a few minutes of asking for an introduction, I got to meet Angie. Unassuming and as humble as could be, she was appreciative that I took the time to recognize her and say thank you for her hard work. We had but a few minutes to speak during that brief encounter, but in that moment, her relational capital account had been opened and a large deposit made accordingly.

I didn't have the opportunity to work with Angie for the subsequent few years, but when building my leadership team for Apprentice University, I was looking for extraordinary individuals who could lead, teach, and adapt to challenges imminent in a startup. It wasn't long into that exercise that I remembered Angie. I spent a few months getting to know her and understanding her values and her leadership capabilities, all along increasing that balance in her relational capital account. The timespan between the first training video for those parents to the date I hired her was approximately three years – a long interview, to be certain. I'm pretty confident that she didn't expect that little video to turn into a really challenging leadership role with Apprentice University.

CHAPTER THREE

NETWORKING

I f you want to be successful in any field, it's essential that you are able to build rapport and intentional relationships with others. Networking is an art, and those who have perfected its practice know that it all comes back to a mindset of respect and service.

How do you convey your strong character and your competence when interacting with others? In this chapter, we'll discuss the different attitudes you should have as you network if you want not only to leave a lasting good impression, but also to live with kindness and respect.

Character, authenticity, selflessness, and a strong network are the foundational ingredients to being intentionally extraordinary.

Character, authenticity, selflessness, and a strong network are the foundational ingredients to being intentionally extraordinary.

Seek to Learn

Networking is not a visit to the ATM, nor is it a drive-thru window. Rather, consider it the headwaters of a possible long-term relationship. Now, certainly, not every networking meeting will produce your new best friend, but that ought to be the mindset with which you enter conversations. Your goal during networking, even if you were asked to meet, is to know and understand the other person. You never know where a simple networking conversation might lead or who the other person knows that might benefit you. You're expanding your network and each networking interaction with your network needs to be intentional and deliberate.

You've undoubtedly met the guy who knows it all, right? He finishes your comments and seems hell-bent on making you feel insignificant. Remember, we talked about this guy when we explored the character trait of hubris. Now that you have a mental picture of this person and know how *not* to behave, let's explore for a moment the benefits you accrue by entering into a networking conversation when you first seek to learn.

Intentionally seeking to learn from others includes:

- Focusing on the person with whom you're meeting – no eye wandering or interruptions. Be in the moment.

- Silencing your phone and turning it upside down, out of your reach. Don't grab for it.

- Knowing the person – their expertise, credentials, strengths, and profession, in advance of your arrival. It will make for a richer and more fruitful conversation.

- Demonstrating your trustworthiness (more on this later).

We all want to network with people who are well connected in our communities. These people are busy – *very busy*. One of my employees asked me to meet with a friend of hers named Ali. Of course, that's an easy decision. My crew guards my calendar and knows the value of meeting time. I committed to meeting with Ali for 30 minutes. The meeting was scheduled several weeks out and, as usual, both sides of the brief meeting were booked pretty solid. Because Ali was the friend of one of my staff, I was eager to spend a few minutes with her both to get to know her (the person receiving the request for networking ought to consider it an honor to be asked – and I did) and, a bit selfishly, I wanted to know the company my employee keeps.

Ali arrived just about ten minutes after the designated start time of our meeting. She seemed like a nice young lady who was just getting started in her career. Apparently no one had discussed the importance of punctuality and the etiquette around networking. Without an apology for her tardiness, she pulled out her resume and a list of about two dozen companies for whom she wanted to work. It was a bit overwhelming. I was hopeful our conversation would be something along the lines of coaching or career advice – something I could start and complete in just a few minutes together. Even a few introductions here and there where Ali might network would have been just fine, but sadly, Ali's agenda was very different. She didn't arrive prepared to learn and eager to be in the moment. Rather, she proceeded to ask me who I knew in each of the companies she had on her list. I was given little opportunity to ask questions, get to know her, or provide any level of advice whatsoever. I found myself eager to conclude this conversation as quickly as possible and resume my other responsibilities. Ultimately, I connected Ali with a friend at one of the companies on her list, albeit with a caveat, and somewhat reluctantly. Ali's relational capital account with me was near zero. A mindset of learning and questions over requests would have produced a different balance in Ali's account.

But, there's a twist… be cautious for whom you request time on a person's calendar. Your request for time on a busy person's calendar for a friend reflects you. In this case, Ali's lack of preparedness and behavior stunned my crew member. I certainly didn't attribute this to my employee, but had it been with someone else, her reputation would have been dinged a bit.

Recently, I was scheduling a networking meeting with my long-time friend Paul. He was very courteous, thoughtful, and thankful in scheduling. I found this refreshing, as such traits are somewhat uncommon these days. As usual, my calendar was rather difficult, and he willingly offered to meet in my office to respect my inflexible calendar. When scheduling, he politely communicated with my assistant and replied in a timely fashion. Knowing we only had forty-five minutes, he arrived five minutes early and intentionally sought to wind up our meeting five minutes before the established end-time. He was an experienced professional who knew the value of one-on-one time. He brought to the meeting a one-page summary of his goals for our time together, giving us specifics to discuss. He was eager, focused, and determined to learn. One of the items on Paul's agenda was to assist him in thinking through some job and career changes he was facing. Paul was quite prepared and we made the most of our few minutes together. While I didn't have an opening on any of my teams for my friend, I certainly was assessing the question every Talent Spotter considers when networking: Can I, with confidence, refer this person within my network? Paul passed with flying colors – and given his experience, I'm pretty sure he *did* expect that.

Build Trust

Trust is essential and people want to work with individuals they trust. Networking is all about starting and building trusting relationships. Not all your networking relationships must be deep, but they must be intentional. Experienced professionals and Talent Spotters see right through the facade of networking for the purpose of just meeting volumes of people. Networking in this context usually results in shortened meetings.

Remember, if you ask a Talent Spotter for their time, you have an opportunity to learn and build trust. No professional will go out of their way and make key introductions for you – and use their relational capital with their friends – if they don't trust you. Building this trust may take several conversations, so be cautious about asking for referrals too quickly. If you are fortunate to take anything from the meeting, anything at all, make a note of it. Use that material for your subsequent thank you note.

Lance was an accomplished businessman, referred to me by a trusted friend. With years of rich experience, he was quite accomplished in his field. As Lance's background was in a field in which I had interest but little experience, I was eager to meet him. We had many mutual friends, and we had previously met, but we did not know one another very well. Lance wanted to discuss how to transition his career into the technology sector. Our conversation was thoughtful and he, being experienced at networking, knew I would gladly provide referrals and references if we could build the necessary yet unspoken level of trust. Our meeting was but twenty minutes old when it was evident we were on the same page. I was able to connect Lance with a few key individuals he was seeking to know. Such was the level of trust and his desire to learn more about me and my businesses that he asked if he could connect me with his previous employer. Lance landed a great job with a great company, smack in the middle of his desired career path. I am thankful to have been part of that networking journey for him. This is not an uncommon occurrence when working with professionals you trust. When I think about networking and trust, I cannot help but think of my friend Nikki Lewallen. Those of us who are fortunate to know Nikki truly appreciate the authenticity and trusted relationships we have with her. Nikki is no ordinary professional with respect to networking. In fact, Nikki's business is a platform upon which professionals engage with one another for high-value networking. A chapter in this book on networking and, in particular, building trust, would be incomplete without some of Nikki's insightful wisdom. Nikki kindly shared some profound thoughts with me about networking and trust:

> "Networking is such a critical skill and one that is oftentimes overlooked. The ability to build lasting

relationships is an art and one of the most valuable and transferrable skills that you could ever have. I can't overemphasize enough how important it is to be selfless and intentional in your networking. Invest your time and energy into the <u>right relationships</u> and do whatever it takes to help them succeed. I have a couple of suggestions to ensure that you are successful in building relationships. First, keep your word. Follow through on what you say you will do and even try to exceed expectations. Second, be a great communicator. I am constantly reminding my staff to over communicate. And, third, be authentic. Share yourself with your relationships. Find as many commonalities as possible to build deeper relationships and oftentimes that includes sharing failures and challenges.

"As you build your network, never stop connecting with new people. Remember, stay intentional and focus on the right relationships that are strategic. When I define strategic, I say 'win-win.' Find a professional networking organization that aligns with your values and goals and get involved. Taking a leadership role could be a great system for you to consistently build new strategic relationships."

Give First

There's a networking group named Business Networking International, or BNI, as they call themselves. They have many chapters throughout the world. Dennis Dunn, a good friend and recent president of a chapter that meets at my office weekly, introduced me to this group. I find these BNI groups intriguing for several reasons. First, they are super intentional. They measure everything and are adamant on making connections for one another, but most importantly, they seek to give without any expectation of ever receiving. Theirs is a selfless, others-first mindset that is pervasive throughout their programming, meeting agendas, and members. How refreshing!

I meet with my friend Dennis whenever the opportunity arises. Dennis, and all the other BNI members, understands the intrinsic value of relational capital. We swap networking requests and favors all the time, but every time Dennis meets with me, he asks: "What might I do for you today?" This is rare, and it's even somewhat awkward to come unprepared for this question – of which I am often guilty. Dennis's extraordinary and intentional efforts toward giving always make him come to mind first when I think about quality introductions.

There is no scoreboard nor ledger on how often or how many times you can help someone with a networking connection.

Like Dennis, when seeking to serve others first, it's important to never keep a ledger or a scoreboard. There is no scoreboard nor ledger on how often or how many times you can help someone with a networking connection. Now, this may seem trivial to the more seasoned professional reading this book, but this little expectation of networking isn't taught anywhere.

After meeting with a young man, Eric, off and on for a few months, he requested an introduction to a very wealthy friend of mine. Eric was a nice guy, but I wasn't confident he was ready for this meeting nor that he wouldn't damage my relationship with my friend. I kind of danced around saying "no" for a little while until he said, "Look, I've given you six referrals and you've provided me with only four. You owe me." I'm confident my facial expression adequately demonstrated my puzzlement and probably a bit of frustration after hearing this comment. Clearly Eric didn't understand that you don't keep score. I didn't connect Eric to my friend and I stopped spending precious time with Eric after this rather awkward demand. Sadly, Eric overdrew his relational capital account with me with just one statement (demand). By now, you know how this story ends…

Quality First

The "quality" of a networking introduction directly reflects the character of the giver. Some people are very well connected and understand the networking engagement rules of listen, give first, and provide quality referrals. Few referral givers will expose their friends to knuckleheads.

My good friend Kim Stoneking is a man of deep character. He is a master at creating high-quality, intentional, and impactful networking referrals. He is a machine! His networking connections are always of the highest usefulness to my businesses. Kim most certainly doesn't keep a ledger, or else I'd be way upside down in my account balance. He makes it a point to both continue to intentionally expand his professional network while intentionally giving away, without expectations, game-changing referrals.

In the course of preparing this book, I had an opportunity to have coffee with Kim and I asked him about his motivations regarding prolific networking and referral-giving behaviors. I had an opportunity to do a little interview with Kim during our time together:

> "The advice I got from one of my mentors early on after going full time with my executive coaching business was, 'Don't waste your time with networking. It's not worth it.' He went on to explain that the people you meet will just take from you, and give nothing in return. Glad I decided to test it out before taking his advice. Networking quickly became a regular activity and was and still is a large source of business for me. My mentor was right about one thing: there are a lot

of "takers" out there, but you get used to it. It just goes with the territory.

"The key is to not keep score. Take advantage of every opportunity to give with no expectation of getting anything in return. Read that sentence again. Make it a goal for yourself to give more than you receive. There is not a doubt in my mind that there are a number of individuals to whom I have given connections that have led to business for them and I have never gotten anything back. Since that's my goal, I find that rewarding and the focus is where it belongs. I've also received referrals from individuals with whom I have not had contact for as long as six months or more. An opportunity arises, they remember me and how I gave to them, and then it comes back to me with a warm referral.

The key is to not keep score. Take advantage of every opportunity to give with no expectation of getting anything in return.

"A client recently shared with me that while he had joined a number of networking groups, he was beginning to question the value. He reported that he has received no new business from his involvement. When I asked how many connections or referrals he has given since joining, he responded with, 'very little.' I told him that he cannot expect things to change if he is not first a giver. Give and you shall receive.

"Set a weekly goal for yourself and keep track of introductions and referrals. Personally, my goal has always been eight per week, and I'm darn good at hitting it. Over the years, my 'A' team – those individuals with whom you develop strong strategic relations – has come together, but I still make it a habit to give to people I meet outside that circle.

"One more thing on giving. I made reference to introductions and referrals. They are not the same. If you tell me you are wanting to meet accountants, I may offer to introduce you to a number of accountants that I know. It is then up to the accountant to accept that introduction and make connection with you. That is an introduction. On the other hand, if you tell me you are unhappy with your accountant and want to meet a good accountant to hire for your business, then I may respond with a 'referral' to one or more accountants with whom you can meet.

"I mention this because a lot of people share with me that they don't have the opportunity to make referrals. What I find is they are waiting for an opportunity to make that warm referral. Be willing to make introductions. It would be hard to count the number of times a person has come back to me and thanked me for an introduction because it turned into business for them or possibly led to a referral. What looked like a casual introduction ended up ringing the cash register."

Keep Notes

Power networking events such as receptions, dinners, fundraisers, and such, are quite common in the business world. If you're a young professional, you should take advantage of these types of events as often as possible to maximize your network early in your career. At events, it's inevitable that you will encounter lots of people whose names you'll likely forget the following day. Here's a little trick: keep a pen handy and on the back of their business card, jot down something unique about the individual. If you have a follow-up commitment with them, write it down. After the event, make sure you follow up with this individual with a simple email. If you believe you might be able to help your new acquaintance in some fashion, ask to grab a quick networking meeting (remember, you're seeking to give first, get maybe…) to close the loop.

Oftentimes I exit a networking event with a dozen or so business cards and commitments to follow up. I know from personal experience how hard it is to follow up and connect afterward. Practice and discipline in this area helps, and don't underestimate the difficulty in successfully achieving a timely follow up. But keep accurate notes!

I attended a political fundraising event one evening a few years ago. The place was packed with a lot of people with deep pockets and I was fortunate to know about half of the attendees at this event. Obviously, on the business scene, this was the place to be on this particular evening. As always, I had a couple dozen business cards in my pocket, a pen, and a little notepad to take notes should I wish to make a commitment needing follow-up. As attending the event was expensive, I intentionally made the most of my investment and time. Several of the attendees were on a fundraising committee for this political candidate. I knew I was a target – I get the rules of engagement.

Apparently one young man named Harry was not paying too close attention to the details of his conversations. He was a nice guy and this campaign was clearly a resume building step for him. Smartly, he knew he would meet lots of well-connected people by volunteering for this role. He eagerly discussed with me a commitment to give (yet more) money to his candidate as this was, as they all are, a highly-competitive race. His candidate, of course, was being outspent, as is always the case. I kind of liked this guy and thought he might be molded into an open position I had at one of my businesses – remember, Talent Spotter. During our brief conversation, we exchanged business cards and talked for a moment, and I committed to receiving a follow-up call from him. This is pretty much standard operating procedure for fundraising events – no surprise. The surprise was in the call I received the following day. He must have mixed up his notes. When he called, he failed to ask me to consider a donation, then proceeded to ask me when I might introduce him to my daughter. Now, there are several problems with this scenario: first, he failed to ask for a donation; second, he was seeking to get first, not give; and third, I have two boys and no daughter. I removed him from my candidate list.

Follow Up

Thank you notes are the currency of networking. They need to arrive at your new acquaintance's desk within three business days of your meeting. In your note, spend a moment recalling something of significance you took away from the meeting and reiterating a commitment you made, but always say thank you. A simple thank you note will cement and codify the trust and comfort level you built during your networking meeting.

Back in the days of old, but not really that long ago, there was a unique way to thank someone for their time – a handwritten letter. Now, I know the idea of a handwritten letter is to a text message as north is to south, but here's the deal: it will be read. Every so often someone will send a handwritten letter to me as a thank you note and I always read it twice. I'm usually shocked just to receive a simple follow up email, but a handwritten letter is a rarity. Regardless if you write a letter or a card, it must be handwritten. Handwritten notes are much more personal and demonstrate you care enough to take the time to think about and reflect on your conversations.

Show Respect

When networking, listen intently and be in the moment, completely and emotionally attached to the conversation at hand. In this chapter, we've discussed some key elements of networking, but I'd be remiss not to mention a few behaviors that will cause a Talent Spotter to exit your networking meeting altogether.

Showing respect for those with whom you're networking is crucial. Remember, you not only represent yourself, but if a mutual friend connected you to someone, you represent that friend as well. This is a big responsibility and if you blow it, it's likely that your mutual friend will hear about it. Few things are more annoying than to have carved off a valuable slice of time for someone only to have them waste it. For example, two guys who wanted some advice and counsel on starting their business requested a meeting with me. Like other networking opportunities I've discussed in this book, I found the invitation humbling and I agreed to meet over lunch. We were but minutes into the conversation when one of the guys got up to take a phone call. I just assumed it was his wife or something, but I was disappointed to hear him tell his business partner they didn't get a deal they had been pursuing. Now, perhaps that was the biggest news of their year, but I found it odd he would exit our meeting for a call – without an apology. Right after we finished eating our lunch, he started texting feverishly and never bothered to re-engage in our conversation.

I truly wanted to help these guys and during our conversation I had mentally prepared a short list of introductions from which they would benefit. But after the texting saga, I was reluctant to share my network with these guys for fear of damaging my relationship with my friends. My intuition alarm bells were going off loud and clear – don't get burned by connecting these guys to your friends. I didn't have the heart to tell the guy who remained engaged in the conversation that his buddy had trounced my referrals.

Body Language

Earlier in this chapter, we discussed earning trust and seeking to learn. As much as your words and eye contact influence the person with whom you're meeting, your body language tells a lot more. Your eyes might look intent, but if your body language screams, "I can't wait to get out of here!", then your networking opportunity is over. There are many great books on body language dos and don'ts so we will not dive too deeply into this subject, but I'd like to touch on a few key points of consideration.

Just like there's no crying in baseball, there's no yawning in networking. Yawning in a networking meeting, or worse in an interview, is a complete and utter *faux pas*. If you must, load up on coffee or soda prior to your meeting...whatever you must do – but never, ever yawn. In the middle of an interview with a college-age student one day, he started yawning. He yawned not once, not twice, but more than fifteen times. For fun, one of our guys kept a tally. If you know you're more awake in the mornings than the afternoons, keep your meetings in the mornings. Yawning in a meeting sends an incredible signal of boredom and disrespect. This young man didn't get the job he was seeking. After he learned why, he was shocked and totally unaware he was yawning. Obviously, he wasn't expecting that, but he will the next time.

Remember when your grandmother used to say, "Put all four legs of that chair on the floor!"? Well, Granny was right – straighten up. Nothing sends a message of immaturity faster than slouching in your chair or leaning back on two legs. Surely these rules are review for you and you're rolling your eyes, thinking, "Really, Ron, you're dragging me through how to sit in a chair?" Well, yes, I am – because I see silly chair behavior all the time. Perhaps Granny's Rule has long since been forgotten, but she had it right. There are many social and professional norms – let's call them unwritten rules – by which business runs, and professionals, especially Talent Spotters, are watching to see if you heed those rules. Talent Spotters are eager to consider you for an interview, but likewise, they're looking for reasons to quickly dismiss you from consideration and save themselves precious time.

> *Talent Spotters are eager to consider you for an interview, but likewise, they're looking for reasons to quickly dismiss you from consideration and save themselves precious time.*

I'll conclude this chapter with an embarrassing story so you won't forget Granny's Rule. I was meeting with a prospective employee named Ginger at a local coffee shop. This coffee shop has tall bar stools well situated for intentional networking meetings. They also have soft chairs and couches, but those types of seats are off limits for networking and interviews. Unless you are close friends with the person you're meeting, those chairs should be considered taboo. Those cushy chairs are far too casual *and* they attract yawns. Ginger arrived, dressed nicely and obviously well prepared for our meeting. We found a table with two bar stools. During our meeting, surprisingly, she kept leaning back in her chair, breaking Granny's Rule. We were about fifteen minutes into our meeting when she tipped the stool over backwards. On the way down, her chair caught the back of another vacant chair, preventing her from splattering on the floor. Thankfully, she wasn't hurt, but to say she was embarrassed would be a gross understatement. Coffee shops are popular places for networking these days. Remember the two coffee shop networking rules: no cushy chairs, and Granny's Rule.

Some reading this chapter will think I'm making too big a deal of the importance of preparedness and behavior in networking. I suggest that in an economy that runs on relational capital, blowing a business or job opportunity due to sloppiness in networking is far more common than presently measured, and it is very costly.

CHAPTER FOUR
COMMUNICATIONS

COMMUNICATIONS

Talent Spotters notice the method, frequency, and eloquence with which you communicate. Subtle things like how you write the salutation, (did you know there was such a thing? We'll cover that in a little bit), the signature line in the footer of your email, or your disposition in a voicemail all reveal a lot about you. Even the font style you use in your email contributes to the reader's mental image of you. Professionalism displayed in your communications day in and day out *slowly* ratchets up your reader's perception of your character and personal brand. Conversely, one poorly written message can easily deplete your relational capital. Now, I sure don't want to put you on pins and needles causing you to run every email you have through Grammarly[4] before hitting send – that would be foolish. But, it is evident that this book must include some basics about business communications. Get it right and you impress Talent Spotters.

Let's dive into some key elements of communications, specifically the confluence of business communications, etiquette, and job seekers. Because the phone and email are such integral parts of communications these days, we'll focus much of this chapter on preparing you to write extraordinary and impressive communications.

---

[4] www.grammarly.com

Timeliness

Of course I had to lead this chapter off by discussing timeliness in communications. If you were a student of mine in the past ten years, you know my disposition about timely communications. Email is both a blessing and a curse, a wonderful tool and a stinking nightmare, a great method for communication and the worst method for communication. How can a technology that's been around for twenty-five years still be so doggone difficult today? I'm not talking about the technology behind you sending and receiving your email, but rather the encumbrances this fundamental method of communication represents and shoves into our lives. Obviously, the first problem with email is that there's too much of the stinking stuff. Like the nasty vine kudzu, you can delete it from your inbox, but the next morning it's all grown back again. High volumes of email cause us fatigue and we lose interest in the handling of this crucial but annoying communication method.

> *Of course I had to lead this chapter off by discussing timeliness in communications. If you were a student of mine in the past ten years, you know my disposition about timely communications.*

Employers, customers, and Talent Spotters all expect a professional level of communication. I've recently heard some students remark, "I don't much care for email so I just don't use it." Sadly, people with this attitude have self-selected to exit the job market, or shortly will be shown the door. Love it or hate it, email and phone calls are here to stay and you simply have to get accustomed to these tools.

Timely responses to email speak volumes about a person. A timely response conveys respect to the sender. It tells them you care about their time and the care they put into writing to you. Conversely, delayed responses tell the sender they aren't important. Today, no response whatsoever to an expected email or one due a response from you is akin to telling the sender to pound sand. Of course we all get busy and sometimes things back up. That's expected and natural, but it's merely an excuse. In the footer of my email, I stake my claim on the timeliness of responses to email. It reads, "Out of respect for you and your time, I make every effort to respond to your email within one day." In case you're wondering, yes, it's rather trying to keep this commitment. People with whom I communicate know I take their communications seriously. Generally speaking, a good rule of thumb regarding timeliness is to not let the sun go down again before responding to a message. I promise, Talent Spotters will make mental notes about your communication timeliness.

> *A good rule of thumb regarding timeliness is to not let the sun go down again before responding to a message.*

Phone and Voicemail

Do you think the phone and voicemail are tools of yesteryear? Well, not so fast. Sure, voice mail is far less common today than just a few years ago, but it remains a valuable tool for business communication. The nice thing about voice mail is that it enables the sender to convey tone and sentiment, something not available in email or text. Like email, timeliness in your response is equally crucial. Simply not responding to a voicemail is never acceptable in business…even for those phone calls you don't want to return. When leaving a voicemail, keep it succinct. Leaving lengthy instructions that require the receiver to transcribe your message is inconsiderate. Unless you're invited to respond by text message, it's appropriate to respond to a voicemail with a phone call.

Hey Talent Spotters: Don't blow off your candidates by not following up with them even if you're not going to make an offer. It's simply rude, and it damages both your personal brand and the brand of your firm. You give other Talent Spotters a bad rep. From Mayberry to Manhattan, every city is a small town and you just might find yourself on the other side of the interview table one day.

Since voice mail mannerisms and etiquette seem to be two of those things neglected in common training these days, let's use a few stories to illustrate why the phone is so important. When listening to a voice message, have a pen and paper handy should it be necessary to record details.

I interviewed a guy named Phil for a sales position at Bitwise. During the interview, I made a note to follow up with a few of his references. He provided the customary three, but I wanted a few more references representing his previous co-workers. In a sales position, of course, you are frequently on the phone. To measure his phone presence, enunciation, and articulation (customers he would be calling would be interviewing him by his phone presence), I called him early the next morning and left a voice message. I asked him to return my call in order to discuss the interview and additional references *after 4pm* that day. Phil called at *1pm* and left an extremely garbled list of names and phone numbers for references. I had no opportunity to discuss the persona, or type, of references I was seeking. Phil's interview had gone very well, and I was considering him for a job offer, but his lack of attention to detail made me pause. If he was this inattentive during the interview process, how would he behave in his daily sales routine? Phil didn't receive an offer. When I called him to discuss why, he was appalled and angry...confirming my decision. Phil obviously didn't expect my method of validating his phone etiquette and his lackadaisical attention to detail to cost him a job, which was unfortunate, as I really liked him.

Hey Talent Spotters: Don't blow off your candidates by not following up with them even if you're not going to make an offer. It's simply rude, and it damages both your personal brand and the brand of your firm. You give other Talent Spotters a bad rep. From Mayberry to Manhattan, every city is a small town and you just might find yourself on the other side of the interview table one day.

As previously noted, the phone and voicemail are crucial tools in modern-day business, and even though you may dislike using the phone, Talent Spotters must use them. Last summer, I attended a small networking event where I and a dozen other business owners were asked to connect with some recent graduates to assist them with their networking efforts. I struck up a conversation with a couple of new grads who were just embarking on their burgeoning career in marketing and project management. In case you aren't aware, both marketing and project management positions require significant phone time. Both grads were well dressed, well prepared, and had done their background research on me and the other executives in attendance. They even had specific questions about my businesses. Refreshing! I greatly enjoyed making their acquaintance and was eager to consider interviews or introductions to a friend. During our conversation, the young lady, Valerie, remarked, "I hate using the phone. I never check my voice mail. I have no idea how many messages I have." Gulp. I asked her how the interviewing process was going and she stated, "I've had a dozen first interviews, but none have moved past that."

Yes, because I care and was astonished, I asked her if perhaps one of those countless voice messages might be a follow-up to an interview. Her comment was enough for me to move on to the next group of new graduates. Valerie, with eyes rolling, replied, "Who uses the phone for interviews? I wouldn't want to work there." You just can't make this stuff up... Face, meet palm. (By the way, you might want to get used to this reaction!)

Email

Every business email requires several key ingredients. The structure of your email doesn't apply as much to those messages you forward to your best friend or a close family member, but it sure does when communicating with Talent Spotters. Let's dissect the critical email elements you should consider when writing.

Bill Gates once said, "Pilots like to say that good landings are the result of good approaches." Email is the same. Effective emails depend on the warm-up, the greeting. Thus, emails should always have a salutation. The best way to think about a salutation is to visualize a soldier saluting his commanding officer. It demonstrates respect, attention, and tradition. Some may consider a formal email salutation as old-fashioned, but Talent Spotters notice. In what manner do you use a formal salutation? When can you forgo the formalities and just send an email?

A formal salutation is *always expected* when you're addressing a Talent Spotter for the first time and every time thereafter. It's never acceptable to use only the person's first name unless you are genuinely on a first name basis. For example, if you're writing to someone you've never met asking for time on their calendar for networking, your email salutation should read "Dear Mr. Smith," just as you would begin a formal business letter. Never, ever start your email with "Hey." When I receive an email from someone I do not know that begins with "Hey," I wonder if perhaps the sender is really close to me and I simply forgot them!

As a particular email thread begins to age, it is acceptable to simply let the salutation diminish, or morph into a more casual "Thank you" kind of greeting.

It may sound old-fashioned, but using a formal "Mr./Mrs./Ms." greeting is polite. I like the Inc. Magazine's post "The Single Best Way to Start an Email–and 18 Greetings That Will Immediately Turn People Off,"[5] but I disagree with the author's comment that it's too formal. If you're a student or a younger professional addressing an elder or a person in a position of authority or leadership, using Mr./Mrs./Ms. is simply a sign of respect. Seasoned Talent Spotters will notice such language.

When constructing the body of your email, read it out loud two or three times before hitting send. You'll be surprised how often you discover an extra word or typo when doing so. Remember, in email, you cannot

---

[5] http://www.inc.com/business-insider/best-and-worst-email-greetings.html

convey your tone of voice or your body language, nor can you know the disposition of your recipient at the time they read your email. People often discuss the tone aspect of the sender's email, but seldom consider the disposition of the recipient. Have you ever bumped into a good friend and started your interaction jokingly only to be met with a less than welcoming response? The same holds true for email and it's simply not safe to assume the recipient is in a happy go-lucky state. Bottom line, be cautious about the tone and tenor of your message.

While we're discussing the body of your email, let's explore email length. We've all received those really long, rambling, multi-subject emails that you have to carve off twenty minutes to read. As a seasoned Talent Spotter, it's my experience that the longer the email and the more topics addressed in a single thread, the higher the propensity for drama on behalf of the sender. Drama is for plays, not email or business. If you want to damage your personal brand, annoy the reader, and inhibit your likelihood of further interaction with the recipient, send a long, rambling, multi-subject email. Email content should be brief and address a single point. There are rare exceptions, of course, but most often when a lengthy email is warranted, it's best to write a letter and attach it as a document. I have too many stories to share about poorly written emails and we don't have enough room in this book to share them all.

Your font face and font size selections matter. I know, you're saying, "Really, Ron? We're going to discuss fonts in this book?" Yeah, it's important to understand how fonts work, as they convey maturity, emotional intelligence, state of mind, and attitude. It seems subtle, for sure, but the font you use says a lot about you, and experienced Talent Spotters notice. I'll exaggerate to make a point. You would never use the Disney font in a serious email. I have received more than one email over the years with a script font that I had to copy, paste, and change in order to read. Needless to say, my perception of that individual was challenged from the onset. This is not how you want to make a first impression. The same applies to emojis. For the slightly less young reader of this book, emojis are those little smiley faces you see so commonly attached to text messages. Unless you're emailing a person close to you, emojis are off limits.

Help your recipient digest your email by providing both a pleasing font and reasonably sized text. Bored with this subject yet? I know, trivial, but somebody has to write about it. Mixing and matching font faces and font sizes in an email conveys sloppiness and inattention to detail.

Finally, when writing emails of a delicate nature, first consider why you're using email to communicate such information. Never send bad news by email. Bad news should only be shared in person. If you second guess whether or not to use email to convey a delicate matter, it's best to have the conversation face to face. If in doubt, meet. A good habit is to write your email, go refill your coffee, re-read and then send. Email never goes away, but is archived forever.

Email Footer

We've talked a lot in this chapter about the different elements of emailing – the font choice, font size, how these small decisions convey your personality, etc. Those are all important, and those same attributes carry through to the email footer. Of course, we're really in the weeds here, but it's important to understand that Talent Spotters want to be able to find you and to find you easily. There are few things more frustrating than receiving an email from someone and wanting to give them a call or send them a note, only to realize their contact information isn't easily accessible. The good rule of thumb in new emails and in responses to emails is to include your email address and your phone number. Though trivial, and an idea I'm sure causes much eye rolling, it's one of those crucial little things that cannot be overlooked. The absence of easily available contact information makes it difficult for Talent Spotters to engage with you, and that's the last thing you want. On the other hand, the presence of contact information makes it easy for people to receive a forwarded email from you and to quickly identify how to find you instead of having to jump through a bunch of hoops in order to do so.

Keep your email footer simple. An email footer, while important and necessary, can also be a distraction to the content of your message. A footer that is too busy detracts from the material in the body of the email. Keep it clean and keep it simple – provide the necessary contact information and maybe a link to your personal blog, website, or portfolio if you have one, but that's about it. You don't want to lose the message that you so cautiously and carefully constructed in the body because of an overworked footer.

Texting

You've heard the old adage, "Time is money." If we can shorten the turnaround time on simple communications, we can save a little time. Texting offers us the opportunity to shave a few minutes of time by instantly sending quick messages to others. That being said, nonnegotiable limitations and boundaries to texting exist in business communications. You will certainly drain your relational capital account with a Talent Spotter if your relationship is insufficiently mature and you launch into texting as a primary communication method. It's best to assume that most Talent Spotters consider texting too close, or too invasive of their personal space. Don't mistakenly think that the Talent Spotter is your friend – don't let your professional communications guard down too soon. Texting is commonplace amongst friends, but in the business world, you must first earn the right, or receive permission, to text professionals. Never assume, unless you have permission or receive a text from them first, that you

Texting is commonplace amongst friends, but in the business world, you must first earn the right, or receive permission, to text professionals.

have a green light to text a Talent Spotter. One caveat – this "barrier" of texting Talent Spotters will likely diminish over time. In our little old-fashioned world, Talent Spotters view texting people in positions of authority and those older than us as a privilege, but this view is rapidly changing. Nevertheless, I would caution you to err on the side of formality when it comes to deciding what form of communication to use when you haven't received an express invitation to text.

The assumption is that texting is urgent or relates a message that requires a response as soon as possible. Ignoring your text messages, just like the other communication methods discussed in this chapter, sends a "go pound sand" message to the recipient. If you truly desire to change a communication method, or to discontinue a conversation, it's best to have that dialog in person. I know – that's old-fashioned, and besides, who wants to talk *in person*, right? The passive-aggressive approach to discontinuing a conversation by ignoring text messages burns bridges, causes relational capital account overdrafts, and permanently damages relationships. It's just never a good idea!

When considering speed over professionalism or clarity, always default on the side of professionalism. Nowhere is this more appropriate than when considering the combination of texting, abbreviations, and emoticons (aka emojis). When invited to text someone to expedite communications, consider it a privilege. With that privilege comes the responsibility of making your messages or thoughts clear. The use of abbreviations and emojis, while cute when texting with your BFF, are out of line in business communications. When in doubt, leave them out.

The use of abbreviations and emojis, while cute when texting with your BFF, are out of line in business communications. When in doubt, leave them out.

Like email, you cannot assume the recipient will know your tone or disposition when sending your text message. All communications require a sender and a receiver. Successful communication also assumes both are on the same channel, in the same mindset, or using the same language. To you, sending a fist bump emoji to someone might seem like a little celebratory fun, but the recipient unfamiliar with that icon may believe you're proposing to punch them. You cannot assume the recipient knew you were of a celebratory mindset, so it's best to leave abbreviations and emojis out of professional communications.

To illustrate this point, I'll share a story about a guy named Alan. To ensure you don't forget this lesson, we'll call him "Alan the Abbreviator." After attending one of my talks, Alan wanted to ask me some questions about a business plan on which he was working. He requested to meet with me via text, which I found odd. It read: "Hi Ron. I'd like to meet with u. Ur talk made me think about my biz plan. Will u meet me?" Well, at first I thought this was surely a hoax, but curiosity got the best of me, so I replied that I would be honored to assist him with his business plan and questions. Our meeting was scheduled for 8:00 one morning. Rush hour and road construction near my office made arriving to a meeting on time with any kind of certainty a long shot. At about 8:05 Alan had yet to arrive, and I received a text message which read: "WTF! OMG! This traffic is bad. Be at ur office asap." Yes, this is a true story. (Are you shaking your head?) That type of language, spoken or texted, is never appropriate, and I found it rather offensive. Alan arrived a few minutes later, and I helped him shape his business plan a bit, but the mentor in me couldn't resist a little coaching about his choice of abbreviations. Somehow, poor Alan had never been told such language was offensive and inappropriate. He was appreciative of my little talk. His level of embarrassment told me he didn't expect that.

Perhaps if text messages were like Twitter and limited to 140 characters, the propensity to send lengthy, instruction-rich messages might be eliminated. A legitimate conversation over text is impossible, and simply adding more text into a longer message doesn't make it any easier. A lengthy text might be less bad than a hundred short messages, but the likelihood your recipient will miss key elements of your message is certain. Here are a few good rules of thumb about using text messages.

First, never send bad news via text. It's the wrong medium for emotional content, as you cannot be with the person to console or encourage them when you hit them between the eyes with something stunning. Next, if your message is timely, or urgent, call. For example, if you need to give last-minute instructions or a change of venue for a meeting, your recipient will probably miss the message, as they're likely preparing for that activity. It's a good idea to avoid texting if your message might elicit a question or cause confusion on behalf of the recipient. Asking the often offensive question of "Does that make sense?" doesn't help the recipient understand your rambling. (I could write a whole chapter on the condescending phrase "Does that make sense?", but I'll leave that for another book.) The bottom line about texting: when in doubt, pick up the phone and call.

Thank You Cards

As I previously stated in regard to networking, I cannot emphasize enough the importance of an old-fashioned, handwritten thank you note. Following a networking meeting, an interview, or a simple introduction at a group gathering with a note tells the recipient, "I remember you and I appreciated our time together." Thank you cards which follow an interview should convey your appreciation for the opportunity to explore career opportunities with the recipient's company. Reiterating the highlights of your conversation in a thank you note with someone you briefly met in a note card tells that person you paid attention, you listened to their words, and you appreciated the opportunity to meet them.

Reiterating the highlights of your conversation in a thank you note with someone you briefly met in a note card tells that person you paid attention, you listened to their words, and you appreciated the opportunity to meet them.

Due to their rarity, sincere thank you cards have a lasting effect. By now you've undoubtedly noticed how much I enjoy working with students and young professionals. I have an entire bookshelf dedicated to thank you notes from students I have been fortunate to help over the years. It is a trophy case of sorts. The thoughtful act of a sincere thank you note brings out a bit of sentimentality in me and reminds me to go the extra mile when helping that young person. They remind me how fortunate I am to work with young professionals and they serve to keep that person at the forefront of my thoughts when I hear of job opportunities. Not everyone will keep thank you notes, but rest assured, they last longer than an email and tend to remain on the desktop of a Talent Spotter.

As with all other forms of communications I've discussed in this chapter, thank you notes must be timely. Like a gallon of milk, there's a "best used by" date for thank you notes. If you've ever mistakenly poured and nearly drunk a glass of spoiled milk, you can imagine the similar reaction of the recipient when receiving a thank you note weeks after a meeting. If, for some reason and within a short window of time, your timely thank you note is not so timely, a simple apology for the tardiness may buy you a little grace. After some point a late thank you note is as spoiled as finding a toddler's sippy cup of milk in a mini-van from last summer. I have received thank you notes several weeks after a meeting and since so much time had transpired I had forgotten the meeting - opportunity lost. Needless to say, those cards didn't make my trophy case.

> *Like a gallon of milk, there's a "best used by" date for thank you notes. If you've ever mistakenly poured and nearly drunk a glass of spoiled milk, you can imagine the similar reaction of the recipient when receiving a thank you note weeks after a meeting.*

RSVP

Répondez, s'il vous plait, translated from French, means "respond, if you please."

Scenario: A friend invites you to a very formal black-tie reception at a fancy venue on September 1st. The total cost of the event includes the cost of the meal, the venue, and the speakers' and staff's time to prepare, and is easily more than $125 per person. Your friend obviously thought enough of you to invite you to attend, and plans to spend a fair amount of money for your dinner. The invitation reads, "We request the pleasure of your company to this reception. Please RSVP by August 15th." You review your calendar and decide you can make the event, but you set the invitation aside until later. On August 28th, you see the request to RSVP and hastily send a message to your friend that you appreciate the invitation and plan to attend. On September 2nd, you see pictures of your friend's black-tie dinner as you click around Facebook You forgot to attend.

I sure hope you see multiple ways in which this scenario could have been handled better. First, not promptly responding to the invitation forced your friend to change the number of attendees, seating arrangements, as well as other details. Next, accepting the invitation just a few days prior to the event likely caused your friend a headache and precious time adding another seat. Finally, due to your forgetfulness, your friend wasted both a precious seat and the cost of your meal. The result of this scenario is probably not an "overdraft" in your relational capital account with your friend, but definitely a significant decline in its value. Worse, the message you sent to your friend is that of disrespect.

A long-time friend once invited me to attend a breakfast as his guest. My friend had purchased a table for eight, and I was honored to accept his invitation - the same day I received it. I did not want him wasting time having to loop back and ask again. I, along with six others, showed up on time and took our seats. The place settings and chairs were rather close together as is customary at such an event. Shortly after the event began, a young man named Logan entered and excitedly searched for his seat. The look on our host's face was that of extreme embarrassment, as our table had no extra seats. I could tell he was both embarrassed and frustrated that Logan never responded to the invitation nor indicated his intention to attend. The seat had been given to someone else. Our host politely stood, gave his seat to Logan, and walked to the back of the ballroom hoping to find a vacant seat somewhere, but *not* with his guests.

Most of us at the table knew one another quite well. Many of us were business owners or executives in our respective firms. What had happened was obvious – Logan neglected to RSVP, and this failure caused a very awkward moment. One of the guys shot a glare at Logan that would have caused him to choke had he noticed. As you might imagine, the situation was more than tense, but Logan didn't notice the glances across the table. After the event, our host returned to our table for some networking and conversation (the real value of the breakfast). Logan had long-since bolted. My friend, however, was quite humble and appreciative that we attended as his guests. He never mentioned his (now former?) friend Logan's behavior, instead choosing to focus on the speaker's remarks.

Sadly, such stories occur too often these days. A simple email RSVP saying, "Thank you for the invitation for the September 1st dinner. I plan to attend," goes a long way in helping put the organizer's mind at ease. The simple courtesy of a reply, *whether or not requested and whether or not you plan to attend*, is polite. Ignoring an RSVP sends the completely wrong message to the host.

> The simple courtesy of a reply, whether or not requested and whether or not you plan to attend, is polite. Ignoring an RSVP sends the completely wrong message to the host.

Unbeknownst to him, the elegance and leadership with which my friend handled the awkward Logan-induced situation wasn't lost on me. I subsequently hired my friend to assist with a big project for which we needed some additional client relationship management. I'm pretty sure my buddy didn't expect that the interview had started during that breakfast.

Finally, out of respect for the host, if you RSVP affirmatively to an invitation, make certain you attend. Unless a genuine emergency arises, if you sign up, show up! It's just common courtesy.

Social Media

Abraham Lincoln once declared, "Better to remain silent and be thought a fool than to speak out and remove all doubt." This often-quoted, seldom-heeded statement provides us with powerful guidance regarding how we communicate. Unlike Lincoln's era, when news took days to travel, today, with Twitter, Facebook, Instagram and countless other social media venues, you can effortlessly publish your thoughts and words for the world to see. Add to this the shrillness, or binary mindset, commonly found on social media (especially in *this* election year), and nearly any comment you make will stir up trouble. Even posting a picture of your dog elicits an argument on social media these days.

Earlier in this book, I introduced the idea of "the company you keep." The company you keep – or your friend network on social media – coupled with those little likes, comments, and shares, tell a Talent Spotter a lot about you. One common theme I hear from young people is, "Facebook is for my personal stuff and LinkedIn is for my business stuff." Perhaps you see the world this way, but your activities on all social media networks represent you, without differentiating between your opinion of personal versus business. The reality is, people formulate opinions about you, accurate or not, based on what you share on social media, whether in text, photos, or videos.

> One common theme I hear from young people is, "Facebook is for my personal stuff and LinkedIn is for my business stuff." Perhaps you see the world this way, but your activities on all social media networks represent you, without differentiating between your opinion of personal versus business.

To be clear, the First Amendment of the Constitution of the United States gives you the right to say and publish what you like – provided it's not defamatory, of course. But this freedom doesn't exempt you from applying common sense in how you conduct yourself in the social media domain. Much has been written about this subject, but a couple quick stories may help you remember to pause before uploading that next selfie.

Enter Sean, a former employee. Sean's work was outstanding until one day when he didn't show up for the Monday morning sales meeting and failed to inform anyone of his whereabouts. By late morning, we had grown concerned and attempted to contact him to see if he was okay. After leaving a few voice messages, sending several read but unanswered text messages, and an email or two, we concluded that perhaps he had been kidnapped. Perplexed, but faced with a very busy Monday, we returned to work, figuring it would sort itself out the next day. We were naively optimistic that Sean was in a legitimate yet complicated situation, and trusted he would eventually provide us with a reasonable answer. The following day, Sean's supervisor texted him well after 9:00 AM. asking if he was coming to work. Unlike the previous day, he immediately texted back and informed us he was sick. Mystery solved, right? Wrong! Apparently, Sean had forgotten that one of his coworkers followed him on social media. He'd found it necessary to share his "sick day escapades" with his friend group. No, Sean wasn't sick. Sean had attended a football game and apparently stayed out way too late partying. When he returned to work, we strongly encouraged him to find a new job on Wednesday, not because of his posts, but because of his dishonesty.

In the busy professional world of technology, vacation days are precious. They're available but difficult to get to sometimes, and when you do take the time off, it better count. The last thing most people want to do on a vacation day is work, especially at a manual labor job causing physical fatigue by the end of the day. We once had an outstanding employee who went out of her way to intentionally serve others. It was remarkable how she sought to help her coworkers complete a busy day of work and still finish her own work, sometimes staying an hour or two into the evening (she was *not* a 59er) to complete her own backlog. She was a gem, but I was always concerned she would burn out, and I definitely didn't want to lose her. When she requested for a couple days off for a mini vacation, I intercepted the approval process to ask that her mini vacation be extended a few more days. Furthermore, I made certain her calendar was clear to allow her to recharge a bit without returning to a larger pile of work – thus negating the purpose of her mini vacation. She would never have shared the purpose of her vacation, but I later learned through mutual friends who were impressed with the pictures, posted by others, of her volunteering at a community center in Indianapolis. She later received a promotion due largely to her selflessness and servant-minded attitude.

Body Language

We discussed body language in the context of networking, but I think it's important enough to mention briefly again. Body language – the unwritten and unspoken method of communication – often tells us as much or more about the person than any other method. There are oodles and oodles of books about body language, so we won't exhaust that subject here, but it is important to understand the implications of your body language. For example, sitting with your arms crossed in a meeting, standing with your hands in your pockets in a conversation, or being the last person to shake hands with someone you've just met, all send a certain message. These subtle but impactful cues, to a Talent Spotter, are very indicative of a person's character. Those are the overt and obvious body language cues, but subtler actions include darting eyes that never make steady contact with others – indicating that there might be some untruth in what you're saying. Or, the worst possible scenario might be when you pass someone in the hallway or on the street, and you fail to make eye contact or simply acknowledge their existence. This very noticeable behavior informs the receiver, "I'm above you, you're beneath me, you're not important enough for me to engage with, and I don't have time for you," even if that isn't your intended message. The importance of body language, the importance of greeting with a smile, the importance of looking someone in the eye – it all makes an impact, so be aware of the messages you're sending.

Conclusion

It's the little things and the attention to detail that catches the eye of Talent Spotters and professionals. Timely and well-written email responses send the subliminal message that you're a professional and you respect others' time. Conversely, lollygagging or silence in your communications, whether it's email, voicemail, or text, tells others you're disengaged and do not respect their position or time. Remember Alan the Abbreviator? Alan's reaction to my "what are you doing?" conversation with him gave me hope when I was in total shock. Thankfully, Alan didn't shrug off my advice, but rather took it to heart and genuinely accepted my counsel to knock off the unprofessional and ridiculous language in his texts. Logan could have prevented a lot of embarrassment at the breakfast event had he just sent my friend the RSVP in a timely fashion. Finally, Sick Day Sean's dishonesty and lack of respect for his employer and coworkers cost him his job.

In all these stories, there's one common theme: *respect*. Detailed, timely, cordial, professional, thoughtful, and honest communications demonstrate respect for others. Young professionals and job seekers who exude these character traits are a gold mine for Talent Spotters. I even remember asking an employee once if she had a twin we might hire.

As you contemplate this chapter on communications, think for a minute about the chapter on character. The two are intricately interwoven and, I suggest, those who are good communicators are likely people of outstanding character and vice-versa.

CHAPTER FIVE
CURRENT EVENTS

Few things reveal more about your character, beliefs, values, upbringing, and maturity than your reaction to conversations regarding current events. That reaction often manifests itself in fidgeting body language or an outright sigh of disagreement, providing a peek into your thoughts. In this chapter, we'll explore some ideas about the importance of knowing about and understanding current events.

Knowing about and understanding current events are two entirely different things. Merely knowing that an event has recently occurred is a great start. Having a solid grasp on the actors, the geography, the motivators, the politics, and other details, behind an event is significantly more valuable. Remember the concept of the learning disposition that we described in chapter one? If you recall, we explored the importance of continuously learning, staying engaged, and absorbing knowledge from your surroundings. Current events are a great way to remain in that learning disposition.

Heads Up!

I often hear comments such as, "I don't listen to the news, it's too depressing." Well, I get that, but that type of attitude is not much different than stating, "I choose to put my head in the sand." When I hear these kind of remarks, it makes me wonder why someone would choose to be clueless. Worse, I wonder if this same person would be dismissive to company challenges and opportunities.

James Naismith is credited with creating the game of basketball in Springfield, Massachusetts, in 1861, but we Hoosiers know a thing or two about "roundball". In Indiana, every driveway and barn's broadside has a rim. Our history of basketball is so rich that we have a movie named after us – *Hoosiers*. As a Hoosier, having played for many years and coached my boys' basketball teams, I consider myself well informed on the principles of the game. Hoosier kids know the fastest way to sit out a game, watch from the bench, and be a member of the "Fine Pine Boys" club, is to dribble with your head down. Dribbling with your head down ensures you'll miss the open shot or the assist pass or have the ball stolen by the defense.

Like a point guard dribbling with his head down, ignoring current events ensures you will miss those macro- and micro-level clues in the market or society that could significantly impact you. In today's culture of instantaneous news transmissions, you must remain unceasingly diligent and engaged. Blink, turn your head, or worse yet, stick your head in the sand, and the competition will score on you – fast.

Conversation Kindling

Remember our chapter on networking and the importance of building rapport? Discussing current events can be great kindling for that rapport. Starting a conversation with someone new is sometimes a little awkward, but breaking the ice by mentioning a current event can provide a fantastic gateway into a rich

Some may think discussing current events is akin to discussing faith or politics. I disagree. The difference is that currents events happen to us and around us, and do not necessarily represent our belief system.

conversation. Some may think discussing current events is akin to discussing faith or politics. I disagree. The difference is that currents events happen to us and around us, and do not necessarily represent our belief system. The avoidance of current events due to political correctness is unhealthy for our society – wait: that's for another book.

Understanding how to initiate a conversation, while seemingly trivial, is important. There is a bit of an art to the process, for, out of the numerous current event categories, some are better conversation starters than others. For example, if you are with a group of people who all follow professional football, discussing last weekend's scores is probably a natural conversation starter. However, in a more formal business setting, football may not be the most appropriate conversation point. Instead, business news, recently introduced technologies, world events, and local headlines make for great conversation.

Before leaving this topic, consider this: If you want to become agile and fluent in starting conversations, stick with something safe, genuinely of interest to you. You never want your conversation-starting attempts to sound like a pickup line in a networking setting.

Discernment

The manner in which you apply discernment to the details of a current event tells others much about how you solve problems. Discernment originates from the Latin word *discernere,* meaning "to separate." Discernment is the separation or prioritization between that which is valuable, of first concern, or true, versus that which is not. For example: assume you have two awesome job opportunities before you and you must pick one. You would naturally think through the attributes, pay, benefits, company culture, and location, for each job offer and then, *with discernment*, choose the best fit for you. For things as critical as your career, you would surely use great discernment.

Often in a networking conversation or an interview, I'll float a few trial balloons of current events to measure the other person's knowledge of and discernment about a given topic. You can actually watch the wheels turning inside someone's head as they develop a thoughtful response that's consistent with the intent of the conversation and their individual values. Experienced Talent Spotters use current events to both measure your understanding of the world around you, and, more importantly, to gauge how you prioritize matters in problem solving and decision making.

Often you must act swiftly, leaning upon your discernment, intuition, and experience to help guide decisions. Sometimes you simply must prioritize and decide between two or more amazing choices with little or no time for contemplation.

Why does refining the critical thinking skill of discernment matter? There are only so many hours in a day, there is only one of you, and all resources are finite. Often you must act swiftly, leaning upon your discernment, intuition, and experience to help guide decisions. Sometimes you simply must prioritize and decide between two or more amazing choices with little or no time for contemplation. Your selection may not be just the obvious facts as presented at that time, but the *projected, forecasted, or anticipated* outcome of each option. There's an old adage, "penny wise and pound foolish," which accurately describes someone who, through the lens of discernment, chooses to save a little in the short term despite the opportunity for a larger long-term return. Your ability to rapidly assess a situation, gather knowledge, project outcomes, contemplate choices, and devise an action plan is an enormously valuable skillset, and one Talent Spotters carefully measure.

Mock interviews are fun and generally far more difficult for the interviewee than a real interview, as many of my former students can attest. For multiple years, I conducted mock interviews for finance students about to graduate from a local university. Year in and year out,

I had the opportunity to meet some very bright young men and women and help them sharpen their interviewing skills. Upon arriving at the mock interview, these students were always perplexed to find my little quiz awaiting them. The quiz contained a few questions intended to measure the student's awareness of and discernment about current events. I would simply replace last year's events with current ones to ensure the events had occurred in the past month or so. These story problems included several seemingly random facts and tidbits of information that a student could use to calculate an answer. The students needed a working knowledge of the drivers and facts surrounding the current event or else their answers were flawed. For example, the questions contained a scenario about making an investment for a fictitious company. I would provide real, recent economic and unemployment statistics and ask how a particular current event *might* influence their investment decision. Sometimes the current event was a good thing, buoying the statistics I provided, while other times the events had a seemingly negative impact. Occasionally, I'd throw in a few red herring facts or random events just for fun.

I wanted to know the students were mindful of the event, could use sound discernment, and could effectively articulate a convincingly logical path forward. Tough quiz, don't you think? The way I viewed this exercise was if I wasn't tough on these students, I didn't do my job. Unbeknownst to many of the students, as a perpetual Talent Spotter, I was truly measuring how they handled the quiz and the actual interview. After one such interview, Mandy, a super bright, multi-degreed, articulate young lady, received a little handwritten note requesting she stay after the other students left. Like the other students, I'm certain Mandy thought the interviews were simply an academic exercise her professor required to complete their course. Little did she know I was genuinely interviewing her. I hired Mandy that day.

Sharpened Decisions

Mandy's answers to my quiz demonstrated her alertness and discernment. Her recommendations for the investment decisions were well substantiated by the facts provided, and she carefully described the anticipated inflection of those statistics based upon the events. Mandy demonstrated how to sharpen decision-making using current events. Had Mandy been unaware of the events used in my questions, she would have arrived at completely flawed answers. In many cases, the economic statistics provided would be on a particular trajectory, and would certainly change course based upon the event. Imagine if Mandy had been unaware of the details of a current event that weighed negatively on one of the economic indicators, yet made a recommendation to the contrary.

I enjoyed fabricating those scenarios in my quizzes to illustrate how current events help sharpen decision-making. In reality, we must use current events to help shape our decisions and actions every day. The events may be of a local or international nature, but, regardless, they must factor into our decision-making.

Engagement

Current events also provide motivation and present opportunities for you to utilize your God-given gifts and talents. One would have to have been as uninformed as a tree to be unaware of the events of September 11th, 2001. Those events rocked both our country and the world, forever changing how we make decisions and live our lives. I vividly remember the shock and awe our country experienced on September 11th. The following days were drenched in deep sorrow, frustration, anger, and a unique sense of community. A few days after the attacks on the World Trade Center, President Bush visited the site, made several inspiring proclamations, and made certain requests of the American people. All businesses, in those early weeks following 9/11, wondered how they would provide for their people as we watched our economy come to a dead stop.

One of President Bush's requests to businesses was to focus on their role of contributing to our economy. Our job was to concentrate on profitability, creating jobs, and fueling the economy, a difficult task considering how the country suffered through those seemingly endless dark days. The country was in an emotionally depressed state – and rightly so. I took President Bush's plea to businesses quite personally and seriously. I gathered a group of business leaders, and together we created the Indiana Business Rally, an event intended to stimulate the state's economy. The rally was a huge success, even making national news. Rest assured, we did not hold this event for self-gain…that would have been the completely wrong motivation. Rather, we created it because our community needed a positive, uplifting activity to help remind us that we must continue to thrive. Had we not held the Indiana Business Rally, we would have negated the values of perception, discernment, and instinct.

In conclusion, current events present opportunities every day for leadership and intentionally extraordinary behavior. How you react to current events and how you engage with others helps you grow personally and professionally while accelerating your learning disposition. Being a perpetual student of current events ensures you are better able to identify and are in tune with opportunities to lead both in your community and your career.

> *Being a perpetual student of current events ensures you are better able to identify and are in tune with opportunities to lead both in your community and your career.*

CHAPTER SIX
ETIQUETTE

ETIQUETTE

air warning: this chapter discusses some incredibly basic, fundamental concepts – things that are no fun to read about and certainly no fun to write about, but someone's got to do it.

My sons, as well as many of their friends and most of the students I've worked with over the years, are very familiar with, perhaps even sick of, my saying, "We're trying to have a civilization here, and we need you to contribute!"

In this chapter, we address simple things we expect you to know how to do correctly in a civilized society. Experience has taught me that these items just aren't common sense or second nature for most people. To those who do practice these things, I'm sorry, but to everyone else, read carefully. Behaving without regard for etiquette, just like cheating in golf, makes you stand out (and not in a good way) to those who understand these rules, whereas acting in a manner that corresponds with an acute knowledge and sense of etiquette makes a lasting impression, especially since it's becoming increasingly uncommon.

What is etiquette? The Merriam-Webster Dictionary defines it as, "The rules indicating the proper and polite way to behave." Practicing etiquette means to behave courteously, respectfully, and civilly. Not only is it the appropriate way to behave, it's one of the first signs a Talent Spotter notices when meeting with someone for the purposes of getting to know them better.

Respect

Simply put, respect ought to be the norm, the de facto of how people work and think.

This idea goes far beyond simply following the old command to "respect your elders." Respect isn't an age thing. It's a human thing. Regardless of their background, lifestyle, choices, age, gender, title, or anything else, you should have a general level of respect for every person that you meet simply because of their own humanity.

To a Talent Spotter, the absence of respect, even in the small things, really stands out. For example, I once had a dinner meeting with a couple of people, and while I wasn't interviewing them to hire them, I was sizing them up as potential partners in a business deal. One of these men – let's call him Mac – treated the waitress very poorly. He was slightly demanding and, even more noticeably, he never used the word "please." For example, he said, "I'll take the steak," and spoke to the waitress without making eye contact, instead of more respectfully and politely saying, "I would like the steak, please." Simple, simple things. Mac's disrespectful treatment of the waitress frankly dampened my eagerness to continue to do business with him.

Respect isn't an age thing. It's a human thing. Regardless of their background, lifestyle, choices, age, gender, title, or anything else, you should have a general level of respect for every person that you meet simply because of their own humanity.

In short, be respectful. Not only do Talent Spotters notice your level of respect for others (or lack thereof), but being respectful is also just the right thing to do.

Quitting

Leaving a job is inevitable. Sadly, the days when long-term careers with the same company were commonplace are long gone. Today's definition of long-term employment is only a few years. In today's economy, the pressure upon millennials to find a challenging, well-paying job is immense and results in significant churn. One thing is certain: loyalty and respect from employers to employees and vice versa seem to have vanished.

I recently had a conversation with Cassie, the stylist who cuts my hair. Cassie is the store manager, and, along with cutting hair, she is responsible for helping hire other stylists. She shared with me how challenging it is to find motivated stylists and her frustration at how people quit. In lieu of a professional conversation, many people would simply stop showing up, and quit their job without notice. The additional workload placed upon the staff by the "no shows" resulted in an unhealthy atmosphere, overtime pay for her staff, and added operational costs. One of her former employees invented a rather clever way of quitting. After missing several shifts and ignoring repeated text messages and phone calls from the manager, everyone assumed she had quit. When they opened her locker to gather her belongings, they were greeted with a note reading, "Ha Ha. I quit." Who does that? Sadly, she irreparably damaged her relationship with her former employer and left her relational capital account with her supervisor overdrawn.

There is a right way and a wrong way to change employment.

There is a right way and a wrong way to change employment. Changes in employment, as we've already noted, are inevitable and an expected element to any professional's maturation process. Remember the learning cycle: try, fail, learn, repeat. As the learning cycle repeats, sometimes the next lap is with a different employer. That's life. But, when that cycle comes full circle, and you realize a change of employment is necessary, don't be a knucklehead and blow up the relationship you have with your current employer.

Quitting by not showing up for work, sending an email, or worse yet, a text, doesn't just send a message of disrespect to your employer – it's equivalent to telling them, "go pound sand.". Regardless of whether your employer is a joy to work for or not, stooping to such behavior when leaving employment is unprofessional and wrong. The fastest way to burn the bridge of reference from your previous employer is to quit disrespectfully.

Your previous employers will be asked by future employers to verify past employment. No employer wants to be sued for making derogatory remarks about a former employee. As an employer, I always ask the previous employers of candidates two questions: 1) Did Susie work for your company between these dates?; and 2) Is Susie eligible for reemployment within your company? Now, you may not be aware that these conversations happen (now you are!), but there's also a more passive and unwritten network of employment validation which takes place. It's called "The Network." The Network knows everyone and everything, and operates faster than the Internet. The Network is always eager to provide honest feedback to employers. You can't hide from the Network. It's informal, undocumented, intensely accurate, and relied upon heavily by Talent Spotters.

> The Network knows everyone and everything, and operates faster than the Internet. The Network is always eager to provide honest feedback to employers. You can't hide from the Network. It's informal, undocumented, intensely accurate, and relied upon heavily by Talent Spotters.

For example, I attended a reception for a big wig one evening and had a conversation with an attorney friend of mine. My friend was casually helping one of his clients fill an open position, and he asked me about one of the finalist candidates. He asked if I had any knowledge of her work experience, character, and so forth. While I did not personally know the individual, I knew who did, and it was a matter of minutes before I had extensive information about this candidate. Do you see how The Network works? It's the Six Degrees of Kevin Bacon rule – everyone knows someone who, within a couple more degrees of separation, knows a Talent Spotter. Those people who make up those degrees of separation have real-life experience with a potential employee that, once shared with the Talent Spotter, will either lead the Talent Spotter to believe a candidate is someone worth hiring or not.

As a word of caution, these types of conversations can be borderline gossip, or worse yet, slander, so it's best to just stick to the facts and let the person asking the questions figure it out for themselves. After a handful of questions and queries into The Network, the real picture of a candidate will emerge. It always does.

So, just how do you change jobs? First, give your employer the opportunity to cure whatever frustrates you. Who knows, you might have been in line for a raise or a change of responsibilities. Good Talent Spotters are always asking themselves "What's the next best thing for this person?" (thanks to Wil Davis, my dear friend you met in chapter one, for these words of wisdom!) and you might be surprised by the plans unfolding for your next challenge. Simply shocking an employer, or resolutely declaring to them that you quit, gives them no room to help shape and mold the position you hold into something much more beneficial for both of you. But, most importantly, quitting abruptly or disrespectfully will taint how The Network thinks of you.

Exiting With Excellence

I interviewed a young lady for a position in one of my businesses. Her name was Charlotte. Charlotte appeared to be poised, put together, and a good writer who used the King's English efficiently. She also had a rather impressive resume. After an outstanding interview, I requested a handful of references that I could contact to gain a better understanding of her character. I was really excited to add her to our team. Within a few minutes of concluding our interview, I was on the phone with one of her former employers … and a longtime friend of mine – Joseph. Pause … Joe and I go way back. We had served on a few non-profit boards together, done a few deals together, and had gone on a few weekend golf trips together. Joe and I value our friendship. Joe's a smart guy who'd never compromise the ever-changing employment laws or do anything illegal that might jeopardize his businesses. After exchanging pleasantries and catching up a bit with one another, I asked Joe if Charlotte had worked at his business. After a rather lengthy pause, he said, "Yes." I told him I was excited to add Charlotte to our team and asked if she was eligible for rehire at his firm. Joe's answer was, "Hey, Ron, I want you to know I truly value your friendship." He did not answer my question. He didn't need to. Enough said…Charlotte was not offered the position. Several months later, Joe shared with me how Charlotte left his firm without notice and cost him a fortune during her exit. I'm sure glad I didn't hire her!

Changing employment is inevitable. How you leave a position means everything. Every city is a small town and The Network knows if you burn bridges. Many of my dear friends are former employees who worked hard while on our team and left with elegance, professionalism, and grace. One young man, Bjorn, was part of our team at Bitwise for more than seven years. I took a calculated gamble and hired him right out of college, placing him in some seriously challenging roles for a new grad. Bjorn served us well. He worked in nearly every position in our firm and did so with urgency and excellence in every role.

After many years, the time came for Bjorn's next career challenge. His resignation was a very bittersweet transition for both of us. It was an emotional time, laced with tears of joy for him and our long-time friendship and tears of sadness that we would no longer be working together. Bjorn remains a dear friend and someone I would most definitely rehire should the opportunity arise. He did it right. Even on his way out, he was being interviewed. Knowing Bjorn, he *did* expect that.

I would be remiss to not address the concept of surprises before we conclude the subject of exiting a job. Only good news should come as a surprise. The time to start discussing your thoughts about leaving your existing position is when you have the *first inkling* that you may want to leave, not after you have made up your mind. Professionals let their employers know when something needs adjusted or changed. Harboring or hiding frustration about your job helps no one: you, your boss, or your company. Approaching your boss with resolute and definitive news that you are leaving your job without having previously discussed it is tantamount to delivering bad news with a surprise. As an employer, I routinely remind my employees I will never surprise them with bad news regarding their employment status. I find it inhumane and unprofessional to ever spring bad news on someone. I wouldn't serve bad news as a surprise and I don't expect to be served bad news as a surprise.

> *Approaching your boss with resolute and definitive news that you are leaving your job without having previously discussed it is tantamount to delivering bad news with a surprise.*

Most employers are eager for you to start your new role as quickly as possible, often within a couple of weeks. I understand the urgency, but I also believe in the unwritten professional code of ethics of treating others as you would like to be treated. I cannot think of a professional position that does not warrant more than two weeks to properly exit. The two-week notice "rule" is not for professionals. You are at risk of destroying the relationship with your employer if your role warrants a longer exit ramp than two weeks, and yet most people prioritize the urgent needs of their new employer over those of their existing employer.

How you exit your current job is as important as your first day on a new job!

How you exit your current job is as important as your first day on a new job!

Greeting

First impressions are everything, and the way you greet someone, whether in person or in correspondence, is one of the first things by which they'll form an opinion about you.

Greetings in writing, including email, present the awkwardness of dealing with titles. When deciding how to greet someone, you have to balance how well you know the person. If I receive an email from someone I am interviewing but haven't yet met, and their email starts with "Ron –", it makes me pause. "Hello Ron," is a little better, but just my name is somewhat awkward. Even worse, if I receive an email with a greeting of "Hey," my first reaction is, "Wait a minute, my name's not 'Hey'!" A useful approach when writing the greeting of an email is to say it out loud to hear how it sounds. If it is awkward when you say it, chances are the recipient will find it awkward as well.

First impressions are everything, and the way you greet someone, whether in person or in correspondence, is one of the first things by which they'll form an opinion about you.

When it comes to greetings in person, after you've known someone for a while, you can of course drop your guard a little, but certainly when you're meeting someone for the first time, it's helpful to recite the person's name back to them. Not only does this help you commit their name to memory, it also elevates how personable you're being. The intentionality of stepping up to someone, introducing yourself, saying your name, saying their name back … that's important and noticeable. Even when you've known someone for a while, it is still polite and courteous to say a purposeful hello when you see them around.

Along with the concept of greetings is the importance of eye contact. Never, ever pass by someone you know without bothering to look up and make meaningful eye contact! It's one thing if you're in a crowded place and have already said hello and made eye contact with someone; if that's the case, you needn't keep returning to the same greeting. But when you run into someone you know, look them in the eyes. It is a simple act of respect.

Timeliness

Punctuality is also a form of respect. A person who shows up late to meetings is basically saying to others that their time is not as important.

Timeliness is important in all areas of life, not just in meetings and interviews. For example, I frequently see an absence of timeliness in email responses. It is frustrating to schedule meetings when others take inordinate amounts of time to respond. If you are slow to respond to an email, Talent Spotters will question your interest in their job. If you aren't timely with your email responses, you are implying that the Talent Spotter just isn't a priority.

Timeliness is crucial when it comes to deadlines. If you commit to a deadline, realize you'll be late (things happen), and you communicate such, it's fine, but if this happens repeatedly, the other person starts thinking you simply don't care. Don't abuse grace – when you do, people stop taking you seriously.

Phone

When it comes to phone etiquette, there are a few key principles to keep in mind. First, if you're on a phone call, keep it timely. Set boundaries around it, try to keep it short, and be respectful of the other person's time. If you call at an unscheduled time, it's courteous to ask the other person, "May I please have ten minutes of your time?"

If you know that you have an important phone call coming up and you're traveling or outside, try to find a place where you can make the call in a quiet location. Background noise sends the wrong message to the person on the other end of the line. A planned meeting via phone should include all the same preparatory effort you would undertake if you were meeting in person.

Finally, if you leave a voice message, keep it succinct and leave your name. While many young professionals and students might dislike using the phone, it's often how interviews are conducted and business gets done.

Dining

Simply put, nothing shows your **preparedness** or lack thereof in working in **a professional** environment than your **dining etiquette**. Once, I was at a lunch **meeting with a** young lady named Jane. **I was shocked** when Jane picked up her salad **bowl** and held it close to her face **while** eating. (Resist the temptation **you** have right now for face and **palm** contact - I'm not responsible **for** your injuries.) At the time, I mentally noted that I couldn't

put this person in a sophisticated business environment – all because of her dining etiquette.

Everywhere you look, you can find classes and workshops on dining etiquette. We make certain that our students at Apprentice University receive training in proper etiquette. In training workshops, attendees learn things such as which fork to use, where the napkin should be, and other important etiquette details. There's no reason not to have dining etiquette training squarely under your belt.

> There's no reason not to have dining etiquette training squarely under your belt.

I've taken several people out for dinner as an interview. If you're being interviewed in this way, don't treat it as if it's your first meal of the week or the last meal of the month. Whether the dinner is an interview or a business meeting, eat a protein bar before you go to take the edge off your appetite: the event is not about the meal, it's about the conversation.

Even if it *isn't* an interview or formal business meeting, remember, you're always being interviewed, and you never know when potential Talent Spotters are watching. Not too long ago, I had lunch with one of my staff members and a young lady who had graduated a few years ago. I noticed when she sat how she carefully placed her napkin on her lap, how she set her silverware down, and how she was polite to the waiter when ordering. Her food came out first – maybe two minutes before mine, and instead of diving right in, she waited until the rest of us were served before beginning to eat her own meal. These were all simple things, but they aren't always taught, and even though this wasn't an interview – it was just a networking opportunity – I took notice and was impressed by her manners and etiquette.

When considering how to act while dining, reflect on what your grandmother would do. **Eating is not a race.** If you don't know whether or not to eat the dish with your hands or your fork, use a fork or don't order it. And, of course, never, ever talk with your mouth full of food!

When considering how to act while dining, reflect on what your grandmother would do.

By all means, this is not an exhaustive etiquette how-to guide; these are just some things you need to be aware of that aren't always practiced. Remember, your table manners make a lasting impression.

Dress Code

Remember Elliott, the guy who displayed an utter lack of self-awareness by showing up for an interview at my office in basketball shorts?

Self-awareness is the key aspect of dressing correctly. Experienced Talent Spotters – and most people in general – know not to be too judgmental in different settings. Of course, if you're canoeing with friends or are at a pickup basketball game, no one's judging your lack of professional attire. But you must know your environment. Last year, I attended a formal academic event – the kind where men wore ties and ladies wore dresses. One of the students giving a presentation showed up in shorts and boat shoes, and every adult noticed it. It was very awkward.

A sensitive element of dress code is the topic of tattoos and excessive piercings. It's important to consider the impression that piercings and tattoos give. A friend of mine, Dale, manages the local office for his employer. While he was in the process of interviewing a woman for the position of receptionist, she shared with him that she had a lot of tattoos on her arms, neck, and the back of her legs. Dale's firm wants and needs the respect of their clients and wants to make a strong, good first impression on them. The receptionist is the first person that the clients meet when they walk through the door. Because of this, Dale had to tell this woman that he couldn't hire her for the job. To her peers, the tattoos might not be that big of an issue. But Talent Spotters have a company's professional reputation and image at stake, and such can't be compromised.

Along with dress code comes the touchy subject of modesty. It's a subject that people find difficult to discuss, but one that is of great importance. Like everything else, your choice of clothing speaks volumes about you, whether you want it to or not. Dressing to fit the latest fashion trend or to look avant garde and cutting-edge may satisfy your peer group, but it's not going to impress a Talent Spotter. Your goal should be to leave people with the best impression of you as a person as possible, and that means choosing clothing that does nothing to distract people from getting to know who you really are. If you want to make a lasting impression on a potential employer or Talent Spotter, then make sure the right things are at the forefront: your character, personality, skills, experience, and talent – *not* your clothes, hemline, neckline, or tattoos.

> *If you want to make a lasting impression on a potential employer or Talent Spotter, then make sure the right things are at the forefront: your character, personality, skills, experience, and talent – not your clothes, hemline, neckline, or tattoos.*

When it comes to self-awareness in dress code, you need to know the culture of the industry and the region of the country when considering what is and is not acceptable. Just as you don't want to show up to an interview at a technology firm in basketball shorts, the converse is true, too: if you are knowingly encountering business professionals in, say, construction, you're not going to show up in a suit. Gauge your audience, be intentionally (positively) extraordinary, and be aware.

Speaking

During a recent interview for Apprentice University, my staff and I were helping a candidate student understand our program's expectations. We realized that after just a few minutes, we couldn't continue the meeting. Every sentence the student said contained the word "like" three or four times, and it became so distracting that we couldn't hear anything else that was being said. "Like" is one of those space-filler words such as "um," "so," and the phrase "I mean." They simply shouldn't be uttered. Speak clearly and be articulate with your words.

Not only should you cautiously choose your words, but you should also be mindful of your choice in tone and attitude. Don't interject yourself as a know-it-all in a conversation that's not yours to be had. It's better to be thought dumb than to open your mouth and remove all doubt! Everyone – not just Talent Spotters – would rather hear someone asking thoughtful questions than interjecting their opinions through know-it-all statements.

When speaking, be careful with your speed, volume, brevity, and choice of words and attitude.

Chivalry

Chivalry has become one of those hot-button words in recent years. I hold a simple and perhaps old-fashioned belief that society is better when men, with humility, seek to serve women ahead of themselves. The concept of chivalry extends beyond men holding a door open for women. It's putting others – from a humility perspective – ahead of yourself

> *I hold a simple and perhaps old-fashioned belief that society is better when men, with humility, seek to serve women ahead of themselves.*

and actively recognizing and stepping forward when opportunities arise to serve others.

Everyone wants to work with people who are thoughtful, who care, who are aware of their surroundings and the people they're with. In most scenarios, the guy should be willing to help a lady: if it's cold, he should offer her his jacket, and he should walk on the outside of the sidewalk. And ladies, if a guy offers you his jacket and you're obviously freezing to death, take it!

Chivalry is NOT about someone not being able to do something for themselves. In fact, let's call chivalry what it really is: respect and courtesy. As a Talent Spotter, seeing someone demonstrate chivalry and seeing another person gracefully accept it builds my confidence in both people, because they were aware, sensitive, thoughtful, and respectful – all traits that I want anyone with whom I work to embody.

In short, etiquette is all about acting in a way that is polite, proper, and respectful. The little things you do form a lasting impression for others to take away, and you want that impression to be a positive one. And even more important than maintaining a positive reputation, you'll be treating others courteously. Remember… "We're trying to have a civilization here!"

CHAPTER SEVEN
INTERVIEWING

Y ou received a call: "We would like you to come in for an interview."
Now what?

If you have to ask the question, "Now what?", it's too late. In this
chapter, we'll discuss how to ensure you're never caught flat-footed in
response to a request for an interview. Besides cooking and religion, the
next longest aisle in the bookstore is on interviewing. As such, we'll leave
the topic of how to interview to those countless other books and focus
on the things you can do routinely to maintain a constant interviewing
disposition. Remember, you're always being interviewed!

While this book focuses more on how to prepare for being interviewed
when you're not technically being interviewed, I've been involved in too
many interviews over the years to not share a few stories. After reading
them, my hope is that you'll repeat the good, leave out the bad, and let
someone else do the ugly.

"Practice makes perfect" and "You play like you practice" are two
wisdom-rich adages worthy for you to understand. Both of these
excellent phrases imply a contemplation of routine, drilling, and rigor.
Teams create game plans and playbooks comprised of the strategies,
player placement, timing, the opposition's tactics, and expected goals.

The team rehearses these plays in the playbooks repeatedly over long periods to ensure each team member knows precisely what to do when a given play is called. The game plan draws from those plays and specifically targets taking on and winning against a given opponent. Rigorous adherence, through practice, to the expectations of each play ensures that each team member's timing and movements resemble the working of a fine Swiss watch. There is no margin, or tolerance, for error.

In order to ensure you're not stuck wondering what to do next when you receive a request for an interview, let's prepare *your interviewing game plan*. Your game plan, like the finely-tuned and well-practiced team envisioned above, determines how you prepare for, execute, and succeed with each interview.

Scouting

Perhaps the title of this book could have been *You're Always Being Scouted*. By the time you receive a phone call about your interview, Talent Spotters have already taken the time to do a little homework on you, your background, and your associations. They have undoubtedly looked you up on social media and established a first impression and some opinions. Talent Spotters have a game plan to consider you for an open position within their company. Now your job is to establish a corresponding game plan.

Talent Spotters know the best indicator as to who you really are and how you will actually perform under their employment isn't always evident during an official interview.

There are some questions to answer that will impact the outcome of the interview. Most importantly, how did they find you? If you applied to an open position, that's easy. If not, it's imperative to determine how the connection was made. Answering this question may seem insignificant, but let's consider how important a referral can be. If a mutual friend sent your resume, they are likely in an established and trusted relationship with this company and you can make the most of this referral.

In chapter 3 (Networking), I stressed the importance of quality, trusted referral sources and how their relationships and relational capital balances are bestowed upon you whenever they connect you with someone. For example, if I receive your resume and a note from a trusted friend, that relational capital account balance I enjoy with my friend is applied to you. As such, you, as someone I've never met, enter into a conversation with me with a positive relational capital account balance. Therefore, if your resume reached the desk of a Talent Spotter through a mutual friend, you must enter into the interview knowing the kind of relationship your mutual friend has with the organization. In other words, you were scouted by your friend who was passively interviewing you.

If you received an impressive referral from a very high-profile executive, you are likely entering into the interview with a relational capital account balance few could ever imagine. Your friend has stuck his or her neck out for you and you're determined to make the most of it. You are representing two people in your interview: yourself *and* your friend. Don't blow it like Roger did.

> *If you received an impressive referral from a very high-profile executive, you are likely entering into the interview with a relational capital account balance few could ever imagine.*

Roger and I have been acquainted for quite some time. When we recently bumped into one another at a coffee shop, Roger informed me he was between jobs and looking for his next challenging opportunity. He asked if I would keep him in mind should something arise, a common request to which I always readily and sincerely commit. A few months later, I received an email from a buddy who wanted to hire someone for a very senior position in his firm – a position with a lot of responsibility. From my recollection of Roger, I thought he'd be a strong candidate for the position. He wore a nice suit, was articulate, and had the executive-level experience my friend was seeking. I connected the two of them and found my friend had already been scouting Roger. A week later, I learned Roger absolutely bombed the interview. He squandered the relational capital I had provided him by *assuming* he had the job because of my referral. Now, I'm blessed and fortunate to have many friends, but my referral isn't that weighty. The sad thing is, his background and experiences fit the role perfectly, leading me to believe the job was his to lose.

Roger's game plan for this interview was entirely flawed. He completely missed the importance of listening during the interview and instead loaded his pre-interview playbook with assumptions about the company and his solutions to their every challenge. He so badly messed up this interview that I ended up taking my friend to lunch to apologize for wasting his time.

Fortunately, there are five Daves for every Roger. Dave was interviewing for an executive-level position with a very well-respected company in Indianapolis. The company had scouted Dave for several weeks prior to his requesting an interview. He had two weeks to prepare his game plan and playbook. Dave took the time to scout the company and the individuals with whom he was interviewing via The Network (remember The Network?). With each passing day, my friend Dave grew increasingly knowledgeable of the challenges, opportunities, culture, and executives at this firm. He knew I was good friends with one of the senior executives and asked me to put in a good word on his behalf.

Dave knew this company was facing some healthy competition, as it was featured in the news. Given this and the position for which he was interviewing, his game plan was to go into the interview knowing their markets, product offerings, and competition very well, maybe even better than they did. His research included background of the firm's history, their markets, a summary of their competition, bios of their competitor's executives, assumptions of the competition's strategies, etc.

In order to not appear as a know-it-all (like Roger), he created a cautiously-worded schedule of the assumptions he made while preparing his research. The interviewers asked how he would tackle the challenges the company faced. Given his research and assumptions, he presented his written game plan, complete with 30-, 90-, and 180-day playbooks. Dave's scouting work on the company's motivations for interviewing him and his in-depth research on the competition paid off. His meticulously constructed game plan was unlike anything I've ever seen. Dave could have blown it with superficial research, haughty assumptions, or Roger-esque arrogance in his presentation, but he knew better. He chose to be intentionally extraordinary in his interview preparation and was well rewarded. He landed the (very well-paying) job. He *did* expect it!

Dress

Within three seconds of meeting you, an interviewer will make assumptions about you based solely on your appearance! That's right – the book is being judged by its cover: you are the book and your appearance is the cover. Seems unfair, right? Well, perhaps, but that's human nature and it's unavoidable. You've heard the adage, "You only get one chance to make a first impression." Nowhere is this cliché more relevant than when applied to how you dress and present yourself for an interview. I like the quote from Lady Bird Johnson – "I've really tried to learn the art of clothes, because you don't sell for what you are worth unless you look good."

Your game plan must include how to dress for a particular interview. Note, I said a

Within three seconds of meeting you, an interviewer will make assumptions about you based solely on your appearance! That's right – the book is being judged by its cover: you are the book and your appearance is the cover.

"I've really tried to learn the art of clothes, because you don't sell for what you are worth unless you look good."

particular interview, not every interview. Each interview is different and you need to understand how to dress for each. Determining how to dress for a particular interview requires some research. We're not talking about the level of research Dave undertook to land his high-paying job, but there is homework to do. Your goal in dressing for the interview is to exceed the expectations of your interviewers, but not to be so stiff and uncomfortable that you cannot engage in the conversation. Sticking with our sports metaphor, let's explore the boundaries of interview dress.

On one end, many businesses exist that expect their employees to wear a suit and tie on the job. This is known as "business attire." If the company where you are interviewing has such expectations, suit up. Have your suit dry cleaned, and buy a new shirt and a fresh tie. Don't forget to polish your shoes. This isn't the time to show off those multi-colored socks your Aunt Betty gave you at Christmas. No, this is sober and serious, so dress accordingly.

On the other end is the casual atmosphere. This is where things usually fall apart. If your scouting efforts about a company's culture reveals their dress code is casual, that never gives you license to go below a "business casual" dress standard for your interview. Ladies, the term business casual does not mean you are free to wear a sundress and flip flops just because they are new. Likewise, men, business casual never includes tennis shoes, shorts, or t-shirts. I'm frequently asked what "business casual" means, so apparently there remains confusion on these definitions.

For men, business casual includes khaki pants, a collared shirt, maybe a jacket, and dark (polished) shoes. Ladies, dresses and skirts are always in style, but avoid low-cut dresses or high hem lines.[6] Dress to be taken seriously. If you aren't sure what to wear to an interview where business casual is the expectation, ask some friends who are professionals working in those environments.

---

[6] http://www.wikihow.com/Dress-Business-Casual

The dress code at my firm and most technology firms is generally "casual." Casual dress means it's acceptable to wear jeans and a nice shirt or blouse unless you're meeting with a client or prospective client – then you're expected to step it up to at least business casual. We do not expect nor dress very often in "business attire," so when I meet a candidate for an interview who is all suited up, I immediately know he or she didn't research much on our corporate culture. It would have been easy to ask the person scheduling the interview, but it was overlooked.

When in doubt, business attire should be your default dress for an interview.

When in doubt, business attire should be your default dress for an interview.

I must share a heartbreaking story about Sam. Sam was a recent college graduate recommended to me by a friend who asked me to consider him for an open position. I received Sam's resume and, out of respect for my friend, I scheduled the interview. Sadly, his resume was void of relevant experience, but I chose to remain open minded as my friend's relational capital balance was quite high. To give you some background, the interview took place on a really hot and sticky July day in Indiana – you know, the kind of oppressive heat and humidity that make you feel like you left the sunroof open during a car wash.

I estimated Sam was about twenty-two years old and his suit was about five. I'm pretty confident Sam last wore this suit to his high school prom. The top button on his shirt caused his face to turn red as he slowly suffocated from a lack of air flow. How he buttoned it is beyond me. His tie, while neatly knotted, looked like a noose tied around his neck. Sam had apparently enjoyed lots of pizzas in college. The last time this suit, shirt and tie ensemble saw daylight, he was perhaps twenty or thirty pounds lighter, thus validating the saying "the freshman twenty" that guys seem to experience. Add to this the fact that Sam was nervous and sweating profusely. In an attempt to bleed off some heat, his palms were working overtime and were drenched when I shook his hand. Yeah, we weren't off to a great start in the first impression camp.

I felt sorry for the guy. I did my best to put Sam at ease during our interview, but his constant tugging at his collar in an attempt to pull his Adam's apple out from under the top button was too much for him to overcome. I'm not certain if his inability to make eye contact was due to his shyness (never an excuse, by the way), a lack of oxygen or his mediocre preparedness. Ultimately, I didn't hire Sam, but I subtly encouraged him to do some background research on the firm prior to an interview. Given his condition, I do not believe I needed to encourage him to buy a new suit.

Helicopter Parents

Sometime in the last couple years, candidates started inviting their mothers to their interview. This is perhaps evidence of the proverbial "helicopter parent." A helicopter parent is one who takes an overbearing or obsessive role in their child's life. I'm not quite sure what initiated this interesting yet frustrating trend, but it has been problematic in some recent interviews. On the other hand, it provides for some fantastic stories!

Aside from checking your suit size, proof-reading your resume, or maybe serving as a sounding board for your game plan, your playbook should never include your mom participating in your interview.

Let's get this straight: Aside from checking your suit size, proof-reading your resume, or maybe serving as a sounding board for your game plan, your playbook should *never* include your mom participating in your interview. No, no, no, no, no! Moms, even the lobby of the office building where your son or daughter is interviewing is off-limits. Sure, you can drop them off at the door, but then scoot. No waiting in the parking lot, no loitering nearby.

Me, you, and your mom too is especially common when an interview takes place at a coffee shop. Talk about awkward. It's easy enough to ask the trailing mom to wait in the lobby during an interview, but occasionally I've had a mom resist and insist on being part of the conversation. Yes, this is another one of those *face -palm* moments in this book but I'm not responsible for your personal injury. This stuff really happens. Needless to say, when this does occur, the candidate starts the interview in a deficit.

I was interviewing Stacy at a busy coffee shop. I arrived a couple minutes later than the designated start time, but because I had done my scouting, I promptly identified the candidate within the crowd. Stacy and her mom had obviously arrived quite some time before me, as their drinks were already half gone. I assumed Stacy's mom would excuse herself once we got past the introductions, but alas, I was wrong. This was not my first mom-infiltrated interview, and, being an experienced professional, I rolled with it. Things were going okay with the first handful of questions that Stacy could answer with simple yes and no responses, but when I asked her to tell me about herself,

she paused and looked at her mom. Now, for the record, "Tell me about yourself" is a very common first interview question, but apparently one Stacy needed her mom to answer for her ... which she did! What ensued was an interesting communication cycle that started with me asking a simple question, Stacy looking at her mom, and her mom answering. I tolerated this insanity for about ten minutes (yes, I'm patient) until I had to politely ask Stacy's mom to bug off. Once on her own, it was obvious Stacy's mom had plowed a lot of her daughter snow over the years, because Stacy could barely answer my questions. The interview ended after a mere twenty minutes.

Unfortunately, Stacy's game plan for her interview with me was not well conceived nor her plays well drilled. While closing out our conversation, I mentioned to Stacy that she ought to spend some time considering how to prepare and approach her next interview and that it might be best if she went alone.

Chewing Gum

Don't even.

Biography Page

Warning: I'm about to make the human resources and interview purists cringe and twitch with these comments. You can just tear this page out and move onto the next section if you would like, but this little method of landing with the right company has served many of my connections very well over the years.

Isn't it funny how many Advice Givers there are who are experts about resume formats, lengths, and so forth? I commonly find that those Advice Givers generally are not the ones who decide on the candidates to hire, but rather inform the candidates of a hire/no-hire decision. Oh, the stories I could tell on this subject ... but I'll leave those alone. There are at least as many recommended resume formats and lengths as there are self-proclaimed Advice Givers. With all this advice and confusion, how do you best prepare your resume to tell the awesome story of *you*?

I believe your resume ought not to exceed two pages and should focus on your goals and experience. I see too many resumes which simply state a goal such as, "To contribute to a great team and grow," or something silly like that. Your goals should be well-formulated and equally well-articulated. A detailed enumeration of your experiences should follow your career goals.

Let me stress this point: *Employers want to know what experiences you have and how those experiences will benefit them.* One hundred and one out of a hundred employers will ask you about your experiences. Thus, it is the most paramount material on your resume. Don't make employers work for it. Rather, be verbose and write full sentences. For example, if one of your previous jobs was sacking groceries and providing customer service at the local supermarket, the line item ought to read, "In my role as a customer service representative, I sacked groceries and assisted our guests by loading their cars and lifting heavy items," not, "Bagged groceries, lifted heavy items." Your sentences, or lack thereof, should not make the reader feel as if they're learning a new language known as *Resume*.

> Employers want to know what experiences you have and how those experiences will benefit them. One hundred and one out of a hundred employers will ask you about your experiences.

The last section of your resume should contain your educational experiences, awards, unique attributes, and other such details. If you achieved an industry certification of some type or won an award which demonstrates a prolonged period of rigor, talk about it. For example, if you earned an Eagle Scout designation or completed ten years of 4H, mention it.

As I write this, the 2016 Summer Olympics are taking place in Rio de Janeiro, Brazil. Of course, the U.S. women's artistic gymnastics is one of the most watched and revered teams. The rigor demanded for those athletes to compete at the Olympic level with such skill, talent, and grace is immeasurable. They achieved that level of (near) perfection through countless hours of dedication and hard work. Such dedication and hard work is impressive to Talent Spotters, and they desire for you to bring the same level of dedication and hard work to your new job.

My young friend Hannah's resume demonstrates the rigor so important to employers. Hannah is an accomplished gymnast. She, like the Olympians, trained hour after hour, day after day to perfect her competitive edge. Unless Hannah applies for a job at a gym, the conversation about her dedication to gymnastics would typically be off-limits. Employers simply cannot ask about it unless it is first introduced by the interviewee. What a tragedy it would be if a prospective employer was unaware of her achievements in areas important to her. Rest assured, Hannah's resume contains a clearly articulated description of her success in gymnastics and represents a subject she would eagerly discuss during an interview.

Talent Spotters truly want to know about you, your values, your character, your motivations – what makes you tick – but the boundaries of resumes, and the laws which limit their questions, result in a broad but shallow understanding of you.

To satisfy the sterility necessary for your resume to clear many human resources departments, you really cannot share too much personal information. Interviewers are limited in the questions they can ask you, and trained professionals know those boundaries. However, if you voluntarily provide such information, it becomes fair game for the interviewer, or Talent Spotter, to discuss. Talent Spotters truly want to know about you, your values, your character, your motivations – what makes you tick – but the boundaries of resumes, and the laws which limit their questions, result in a broad but shallow understanding of you. You can overcome this stalemate by providing a personal biography (I just lost my human resources friend group!).

Your biography is *always* a separate document from your resume, or it may be a personal website. Your resume could reference it with a statement such as, "I'll gladly provide my personal biography for you upon request." When emailing your resume to someone, ask if you may include your biography and inform the interviewer you're willing to discuss its contents during your interview. Some may decline to receive it for fear of possible legal ramifications, and, in today's society, that's a very legitimate concern.

Your biography page is your opportunity to tell the story of *you* – things such as your goals, motivations, experiences, and hobbies. I often encourage folks to describe how their hobbies might leave them refreshed and rejuvenated, thus boosting their creativity. A biography page might include a brief description of a book you recently read and how it impacted you personally or professionally. I've seen some biography pages with dog photos, mountains climbed, baby pictures, etc. – all the things you just can't put on a resume. Of course, it's best to leave some things off of your biography page, such as topics of politics and religion, unless you have specific accomplishments in these areas.

When possible, your resume and biography should be tailored to each interview opportunity you are seeking. Review both of them before sending, as it provides you with a fresh look at the documents and refreshes their contents in your memory. Finally, always, always, always have these documents reviewed by a third party – a trusted individual who will challenge your statements.

Game Day

It's interview time. You're ready! You've memorized your game plan and rehearsed each play in your playbook with rigor. As you prepare for the interview, be confident you can answer *why* you want this particular job, *how* you will impact the culture and company, *when* you can start, and *where* this job fits into your goals. Talent Spotters will ask you these questions, so tighten those laces and be prepared. As you ready for game day, remember, an interview is a two-way street. You want to be confident this is the company for whom you want to work.

> *As you prepare for the interview, be confident you can answer why you want this particular job, how you will impact the culture and company, when you can start, and where this job fits into your goals.*

There are a few rules of interviewing I'd be remiss to not include in this chapter. Every book and article on interviewing must discuss these items. First, know the interviewer. Do a little social media research and homework (a.k.a., stalking) to ensure you know what makes them tick. I've actually had an interview or two where the interviewee didn't know my name. Wait – careful…two face-meet-palm situations in one chapter and you'll look like you've been slapped!

Second, go to your interview with at least a half-dozen questions about the specific position, the company, and its culture. A solid set of thoughtful questions tells the interviewer you did your homework and prepared and would do the same for your job when they hire you. Your questions should not lead to discussions about compensation. It's best to leave a conversation about compensation for a subsequent interview. Even then, it's not yours to bring up. That responsibility lies with the interviewer. I could fill another book with stories of failed interviews in which a candidate asked about compensation in the first question or two.

Once the interview is complete, it is appropriate to ask when you might hear back about further steps. If it's not offered to you, ask for an anticipated date and a method of contact by which you will hear from the company. Mark the date in your notes, and afterward, be sure to put the date on your calendar. I like the idea of taking a thank you note to the interview with a stamp already on the envelope. That way, the minute you get back into your car, you can customize the note to the interview. Make certain it then goes in the mailbox *the same day*. Remember, timeliness in communications is crucial.

> I like the idea of taking a thank you note to the interview with a stamp already on the envelope.

Your last step on interview day is to ask your references to send over letters of recommendation. It's best to do this without prompts from the interviewer, as it shows that you are on your game. The letters ought to be short and sweet and, to the extent possible, reference a specific conversation point made during your interview. For example, if you were asked a question about resourcefulness, request one of your references to mention such in their letter. Remember my friend Dave from earlier in this chapter? Rest assured, Dave's references sent their letters on the same day of his interview. I was one of those references.

> When you learn you will not be offered the position, ask what things you could have done in the interview, or what parts of your resume or experiences you may be lacking that would have produced a different outcome. This simple yet powerful question is never asked any more, but it represents a tremendous opportunity for you to learn.

You did all you could. You prepared a great game plan for this interview. You had specific plays well thought-out for any and all scenarios or situations you might encounter. You dressed for success, researched the interviewers, did your homework on the company, prepared solid questions, and had timely references. Despite all this, you did not get the job. Now what?

When you learn you will not be offered the position, ask what things you could have done in the interview, or what parts of your resume or experiences you may be lacking that would have produced a different outcome. This simple yet powerful question is never asked any more, but it represents a tremendous opportunity for you to learn.

Perhaps a better position awaits you for which you need to remain in the interviewing and optimistic disposition. Do not be discouraged. Upon receiving the news you're not going to be hired, your next step is a very formal thank you letter. Forego this step, and you will miss out on an enormous opportunity to build relational capital with the interviewer(s). You should send your letter the same day you receive the news, reminding them you were honored to be considered.

These game-day and post-interview plays will distinguish you from the competition and ensure you behave in an intentionally extraordinary fashion. Once the sting of "no" has worn off from the news that you did not receive the job, take time to reflect upon your game plan, your playbook, the interview, the questions and answers, and the interviewer's disposition. Consider what you can learn from that experience in order to ensure it doesn't happen again in the future.

> *When interviewing, listen more, talk less, and remain humble.*

Interviewing is an art. It requires much practice and patience. Like the Olympic gymnasts, attention to detail and rigor in your planning and preparations make all the difference. Remember, interviews are a two-way street. When interviewing, listen more, talk less, and remain humble.

THE CHARGE

THE CHARGE

"**O**ld guys, teach the new guys!"

The above quote – taken from that classic movie, *Stripes – is a great setup for this charge.* The point that they're trying to make is the guys and gals with training and experience must share with the new recruits. At Apprentice University, we call this mentoring – when those who have been through the ropes assist those who have yet to get there.

After much of this book being directed at those who are trying to gain the (positive) attention of Talent Spotters, I now have a charge for the Talent Spotters themselves, those mentors who know the ropes. Whether you're practicing or retired, your job is not to go on your merry way and resist the change taking place today – changes like employees quitting their jobs by text or leaving a note in the locker of a barber shop saying, "I quit."

There are three different ways in which we can encourage change:

1) The passive approach – live it out. Demonstrate character. Be the example. Show the better way of doing things – in other words, walk the walk. Authentically model the values construed in this book.

2) The active approach – actively engage in teaching and instructing the next generation in why character matters. In today's society, character matters a *lot,* so intentionally look for members of the younger generation to teach, pour into, and mentor individually.

3) And finally, there's the approach to which most self-employed Talent Spotters will likely ascribe: encourage and reward extraordinary behavior and call out the contrary. Praise, encouragement, and shout-outs about a job well done go a long way to bolster confidence in employees. On the other hand, calling out behavior contradictory to the character, attitude, and values we want our future leaders to possess must be commonplace too. To return to the classic example, don't let people get away with quitting by text! Ask for a meeting. Call it out when someone walks into an interview in basketball shorts or shows up with their mom. To ignore them means we aren't doing what we can to prevent their recurrence.

I asked a human resources guru about Charlotte. I described the story of Charlotte, the dishonest quitter. One of the elements we discussed is the conundrum that if I call Joe and ask him, "Hey Joe, should I hire Charlotte?", and Joe stays silent, Joe can get in trouble. Conversely, if I call Joe and Joe says, "No way in the world," then Joe can also get in trouble. There is this catch-22 that isn't for us to resolve here, but if Charlotte embezzled money from Joe and his company and he was to let me continue and to hire her, it would not only hurt our friendship, but she may also get away with it again.

Now, the aggressive approach would be to meet with Charlotte for coffee, sit down with her, and say, "Charlotte, I regret to inform you that we will not be hiring you." This is obviously a conversation to have in person – sending an email for such a serious situation proliferates the negative behavior we are trying to discourage. Once you sit down with her, say, "Look, Charlotte, we could talk about why we're not going to hire you, and we'll get to that in a few minutes, but in the course of doing some background research on you, I learned that you have left your previous employers in a very negative state. I won't share the details of how I learned these things because that isn't yours to know, but I found that you engaged in some improper behavior in the workplace in the past. That's not right, and I feel the need to call it out."

The point I'm trying to make here is that there is a gradient of things that Talent Spotters and the slightly older generation has a responsibility to do, and that's a responsibility we have to all the generations (plural) that came before and conveyed these values and principles to us. The alternative of *not* calling these things out results in mayhem in our businesses – and businesses can't function that way.

Not long ago, I met with a friend who has been a Talent Spotter for many years, and one of the things we discussed was the changing culture of business. He proceeded to tell me that he strives to protect the culture within his firm because businesses as an organization really are one of the last domains of civility. We agreed that if we allow the erosion of culture, civility and respect in business by condoning candidates wearing basketball shorts to an interview, for example, we risk relinquishing that civility forever. How will you manage and grow a business in such circumstances? What joy will there be for an entrepreneur to say, "Hey, I can't wait to start a new business and hire a bunch of people that don't care about our culture or the commitment I'm making to them in the process."

We have a duty, a charge, to fulfill. Our charge to existing professionals and Talent Spotters is this: Be an advice giver with a background that supports what you're saying. You have to walk it, you have to mentor it, you have to guard it, and you have to resist – to call out – the bad behavior. We, as Talent Spotters, have an obligation to the Talent Spotters of the

We, as Talent Spotters, have an obligation to the Talent Spotters of the past and of the future to protect the values that make business run. We can't just leave the mistakes alone and not draw attention to negative behavior, allowing it to worsen and leaving it for the next person to clean up.

past and of the future to protect the values that make business run. We can't just leave the mistakes alone and not draw attention to negative behavior, allowing it to worsen and leaving it for the next person to clean up. We must actively strive to make the business culture better by exemplifying good behavior and calling out what's wrong – to use our experience to teach the new recruits.

This charge is hard work *and* a privileged responsibility. I am encouraged to see some seriously bright talent on the horizon who are choosing to be intentionally extraordinary. I am excited to see the impact young professionals with a "bring it on" disposition will have in our society. I, for one, look forward to working alongside them and sharing some life lessons along the way.

I'll take Charge Option #3, thank you very much... Join me?

CAST OF KNUCKLEHEADS

CAST OF KNUCKLEHEADS

The stories contained in this book, while all true, contain names, characters, businesses, places, events and incidents that have been changed. Any resemblance to actual persons, living or dead, or actual events is purely coincidental. If you're a Talent Spotter and have similar stories from which others can learn, I'd love to hear from you. You can submit your stories on the *You're Always Being Interviewed* website.[7]

- Jared
  - Character > Hubris
  - The definition of hubris: Jared, the young man who thought he knew it all and wasn't afraid to let others know it.

- Unobservant Elliott
  - Character > Self-Awareness
  - This guy headed straight from the gym to an interview.

- Natalie
  - Character > Drama & Gossip
  - Because she loved gossip and drama, Natalie missed out on a job opportunity.

---

[7] http://www.yourealwaysbeinginterviewed.com

- Tom
  - Character > Supportive
  - Rather than developing a supportive attitude, Tom actively pursued the opposite approach. He was untimely, disrespectful, and uncooperative.

- Brett
  - Character > Not a 59er
  - Brett spent more time watching the clock than investing his energy in his work.

- Jaclyn
  - Personal Brand > Resume
  - Jaclyn neglected to carefully construct her resume. The outcome: not the interview she sought, but a polite "thank you" rejection email.

- Kelly
  - Personal Brand > Publishing
  - Kelly supposedly wrote exceptional professional papers, yet somehow forgot basic grammar rules on her blog.

- James
  - Personal Brand > You.com
  - James made the mistake of publishing his past life for the world to see – including potential employers.

- Ali
  - Networking > Seek to Learn
  - Ali bankrupted her relational account capital by coming with a personal agenda and an unwillingness to learn.

- Eric
  - Networking > Give First
  - Rather than seeking to serve, Eric wanted someone to serve him first – and he wanted something big.

- Harry
  - Networking > Keep Notes
  - Not only did this young man confuse his notes, he also collected them for questionable reasons. Wanted me to introduce him to my daughter, which I do not have!

- Carl
  - Networking > Show Respect
  - This guy answered a call mid-conversation, then ignored everyone while he texted during the rest of the meeting, all without a single apology.

- Zach
  - Networking > Body Language
  - This young man caught forty winks at the wrong time . . . during his interview.

- Ginger
  - Networking > Body language
  - She ignored Granny's Rule and consequently found herself in an embarrassing situation.

- Phil
  - Communications > Phone and voice mail
  - Phil forgot the importance of phone and voicemail etiquette. The result was a lost job opportunity and severely decreased relational account capital.

- Valerie
  - Communications > Phone and voice mail
  - Valerie disregarded the fact that Talent Spotters and interviewers use the phone and voicemail; her interviews never went beyond first meetings.

- Alan the Abbreviator
  - Communications > Texting
  - Alan messed up, but took to heart the lesson that abbreviations, emojis, and foul language are not permissible for professionals.

- Logan the Latecomer
  - Communications > RSVP
  - Logan was late and caused a lot of embarrassment. Then, he bolted, and lost the real value of the meeting.

- Sick Day Sean
  - Communications > Social Media
  - Sean shared his "sick day" escapades on social media, then lied about it to his employer. Dishonesty is never a good policy, and disrespect doesn't get you too far either.

- Mac
  - Etiquette > Respect
  - Mac demanded things and never said 'please' to the waitress. His abrupt and disrespectful attitude cost him a business partnership.

- Megan
  - Etiquette > Quitting
  - This young lady played a clever joke on her manager and fellow employees to tell them she had quit. The result: a reputation of disrespectful and inconsiderate behavior toward others.

- Charlotte
  - Etiquette > Quitting
  - Thinking she could hide from The Network, Charlotte damaged her character and reputation by choosing to burn bridges by exiting a business and costing her employer a fortune. That one black mark caused her tremendous trouble in finding a new employer willing to hire her.

- Jane
  - Etiquette > Dining
  - She brought her salad bowl up close to her face, a seemingly small lapse in dining etiquette, but one that expelled her from any professional business environments.

- Tracie
  - Etiquette > Dress Code
  - Appearances matter. She had tattoos on her arms, neck, and legs. As a result, she did not receive a job offer from a company with a professional reputation and image.

- Roger the Referral Squanderer
  - Interviewing > Scouting
  - Roger was nicely dressed, articulate, and had experience. His big mistake was assuming that a referral had landed him a job.

- Stiff Suit Sam
  - Interviewing > Dress
  - Sam did not research the dress code for the business where he was interviewing. The result was an unbearable afternoon in a suffocating, stiffening, sweat-inducing suit and tie.

- Stacy's Mom
  - Interviewing > Helicopter parents
  - Stacy's mom was part of her playbook… so much so that she answered all of the important questions. Stacy branded herself as an unprepared young lady incapable of entering the professional environment or thinking for herself.

Printed in the United States
By Bookmasters